Soft Power on Hard Problems

Strategic Influence in Irregular Warfare

Edited by
Ajit Maan and Amar Cheema

Hamilton Books

An Imprint of
Rowman & Littlefield
Lanham • Boulder • New York • Toronto • Plymouth, UK

Copyright © 2017 by Hamilton Books
4501 Forbes Boulevard, Suite 200, Lanham, Maryland 20706
Hamilton Books Acquisitions Department (301) 459-3366

Unit A, Whitacre Mews, 26-34 Stannary Street,
London SE11 4AB, United Kingdom

Library of Congress Control Number: 2016949332
ISBN: 978-0-7618-6840-8 (pbk : alk. paper)—ISBN: 978-0-7618-6841-5 (electronic)

∞™ The paper used in this publication meets the minimum requirements of American
National Standard for Information Sciences Permanence of Paper for Printed Library
Materials, ANSI/NISO Z39.48-1992.

Contents

Introduction

Dr. Ajit Maan

Given the gruesome nature of extremist attacks on civilians around the world, it seems counter-intuitive to assert that it is not physical force that will defeat extremists, but rather, soft power combined with, and secured by, kinetic capacity. That is the assertion upon which this volume is built.

The adversaries we face now are unconventional and they will not succumb to bullets or drone attacks or conventional weapons. Kinetic warfare can combat the lethal capacities of the adversary but in irregular warfare it is essential to erode our adversaries' power over populations. The weapon of choice in this war is the intangible art of influence.

Some have described contemporary conflicts as a "Battle of Narratives," others call them "Ideological Battles"—the younger version of "Battle for the Hearts and Minds"—but ultimately, we are in a war over influence. Whosoever wields influence wields power. And so far, our adversaries are in the lead.

Military strikes have not been able to combat the influence that extremists wield; even worse, extremists have co-opted our military strikes into their narrative.

The good news is we have the weapons of choice and we know how to use them. The bad news is not enough of us know how to use them, and the few of us who do have been unable to implement widely enough.

Intrinsic to any discussion of influence, is identity—individual, national, and increasingly global. We, as a global community united against violent extremism, are in desperate need of a robust identity narrative that binds together our policies and strategies with those of our allies and places civilian welfare and environmental stability at the center of the story. The institutionalized identity of the United Nations, for example, is insufficient now. We need narratives that live and breathe among people. If we don't craft our own identity narratives it will continue to be done for us. The authors of this book are uniquely qualified to analyze the contemporary security landscape and promote necessary and pressing change. Each is a thought leader in his or her field. Four of the six authors are seasoned military professionals who share the view that the over-reliance on kinetic approaches over influence operations account for some of the failures of nations against extremists. Combined with civilian academic leadership this book is a practice in what Christopher Holshek describes as "military civics." This collection of international perspectives taken together challenge commonly held assumptions and outmoded paradigms of engagement.

Paul Cobaugh provides the framework for the following discussions and in so doing stocks the soft power toolbox by outlining the five Lines of Effort required to stabilize the Middle East. He then focuses on how best to communicate those Lines of Effort to our domestic audiences, to our allies, to our adversaries, and to effected populations, to ultimately destroy the "brand" of our adversaries.

While Amar Cheema's perspective differs from that of Cobaugh, they share at least one common conviction: influence is the key factor in stabilization efforts. The survey of competing international interests in the Middle East by the retired Brigadier concludes by emphasizing that the potential to bring peace to the region will not come primarily through military interventions, but rather, by influencing global public opinion.

Eirini Patsea argues that identity polarization disintegrates communal relationships, even at the global level, by personalizing systemic discord. She locates both the root of conflict and also the place to begin reconciliation, in the process of identity negotiation.

Christopher Holshek promotes an emergent civil-military ethos of service, arguing that "human security" ought to replace the "national security" model and the focus should be on the drivers of instability rather than the symptoms of it. He suggests "military civics" as an operational as well as strategic imperative. American national identity, he argues, should be predicated upon American values rather than American military power.

Christopher Mayer and Farhana Qazi round out the analysis by offering competing visions of service ethos. While Mayer suggests the replacement of the understanding of military service as "selfless" with a notion of "self-fulfilling" service, an identifying characteristic of what he calls "Committed Service," Qazi traces warring words to the supportive service roll of women in extremist groups. She examines the influence of radicalized women's narratives in recruitment and the manner in which the interplay of narrative and identity operates.

Chapter One

Soft Power in the Lead

The Foundation

Paul Cobaugh

Each and every Asymmetrical conflict or insurgency is a custom project requiring a very carefully planned and unique and custom approach that requires employing many non-standard tools, techniques, and craftsmen. The current US *Soft Power* toolbox is half empty and poorly stocked, and we are employing an ineffective antiquated strategy and there are a limited number of true, trained craftsmen.

What we are seeking to do in this discussion is stock our toolbox with more appropriate tools, train the appropriate number of true craftsmen, and enable them with a strategy that is capable of producing and acting on the all-important set of plans requisite to build peace.

Baseline definitions:

- *Soft Power* is any effort besides kinetic military action that can contribute to mitigating, degrading, and ultimately defeating the capabilities of an adversary even when applied in conjunction with military force. It is the ability of a country/entity to persuade others to do what it wants without force.
- *"Kinetic" warfare* is, "killing people and breaking things."
- *Irregular Warfare* (IW), as portrayed in the DOD (Department of Defense) and JOC (Joint Operating Concept) in September 2007, is a violent struggle among state and non-state actors for legitimacy and influence over the relevant populations. IW favors indirect and asymmetric approaches, though it may employ the full range of military and other capabilities, in order to erode an adversary's power, influence, and will. It is

inherently a protracted struggle that will test the resolve of a nation and its strategic partners.

Discussion: We are currently engaged globally in a number of IW conflicts rather than symmetrical conflict against a standing army. One common aspect of all of these specific types of conflicts is that the populace is a significant COG (Center of Gravity). Three inherent truths about Irregular Warfare are:

- Influencing foreign governments and populations is a complex and inherently political activity;
- Irregular warfare is about people, not platforms;
- Waging protracted irregular warfare depends on building global capability and capacity.

While the tools/weapons systems for combating a standing army are numerous, sophisticated, and well resourced, they only combat the lethal aspect of an adversaries' capability. As we look at the three bullet points above it is clear that very few of our weapons systems are well matched to managing these three issues. Every year, the US military expends significant effort and resources to train, exercise, and plan for the execution of Kinetic warfare. However, fighting a standing army is no longer the norm rather but the exception. This begs the question of why we are not focusing the appropriate amount of our training regarding the type of conflict that we can expect for the foreseeable future. None of the authors of this volume are advocating shutting down training for Symmetrical Conflict but only restructuring our training so that it focuses and prioritizes in respect to our current and likely threats.

Special Operations Forces and other Special Operations Forces do train significantly for the Asymmetrical challenges both current and foreseeable. But there are not enough Special Operations Command troops to go around. The folks from USSOCOM are not well equipped for the Asymmetrical fight and armed with a comprehensive strategy and capabilities to ply their trade as they could be. US Special Operations Forces are currently overtaxed and conventional troops are not as well trained, equipped, and armed with Soft Power strategy and capabilities as they can be.

A very large portion of the "soft" weapons most effective in asymmetrical conflict reside in non-DOD government agencies and the private sector who are bereft of the powerful advocacy that resides in the defense industry.

WHY SOFT POWER MATTERS: IRAQ, SYRIA, AND THE LEVANT

I use the descriptor "DAESH" because for a variety of reasons it is unpopular with the Extremists. DAESH an Arabic acronym formed from the initial letters of the group's previous name in Arabic: "al-Dawla al-Islamiya fil Iraq wa al-Sham." I prefer it because it is commonly used in the Levant among indigenous populations and because IS, ISIS, or whomever they are this week do not care for being called DAESH. In fact, due to acronyms being relatively an uncommon usage in Arabic and the fact that when pronounced out loud sounds like an offensive slight, DAESH has acquired some degree of popularity among people offering up condemnation. Why it matters to us in messaging is two-fold; first, it denies them the term "State" when spoken or written outside of Arabic speaking audiences. For those of you familiar with the term/concept "branding," calling them DAESH outside of their home turf degrades their brand. Degrade the brand and degrade some of what is enticing to potential and fledgling recruits. As that the Caliphate and Statehood is the desired end-state of the Extremists, denying legitimacy is important. There is merit in agitating their media effort as that it distracts and diverts attention from their overt, dishonest and barbaric propaganda. Simply put, the more attention and energy they divert away from supporting their ideology the better off we are. There are other reasons in military applications to "provoke extremist media" but I have chosen to highlight these two points as that they support our overall concept of a Communication Strategy. *This section speaks to the "why"* of using select words," such as DAESH instead of IS, ISIL, DAESH, etc. Much in the same vein, when describing a specific individual, "killer," "thug," or "evil-doer" will work quite effectively rather than "DAESH Jihadist" or other such terminology.

In much the same vein as using the word DAESH, we also must avoid using the term "radical Islamic terror." Adding the word "Islamic" to any description of the extremists only helps the DAESH narrative regarding a war between Islam and everyone else. Finally, the word "extremist" by itself is in my opinion an excellent choice. It confers no affiliation to Islam and recognizes all fighters as being outside the realm of normal and decent citizenship regardless of state affiliation. There is even a subtle inference of madness to the word. In the case of DAESH, it works. For many of the same reasons we drop the word "Islamic" when we reference DAESH's terrorism we must also stop using the term Caliphate. The point again is to detach DAESH or the extremists from any sense of legitimacy. The "Caliphate" in reality represents to many the "golden age of Islam" for many potential recruits and by continuing to broadcast that the extremists are pursuing/ establishing a Caliphate then we are helping them market to the Muslim Community or Umman the powerful allure of a reacquisition of glory. Words matter!

DAESH draws support from—and inflicts severe injury on—all associated civilian populaces. DAESH is a media influence effort supported by arms and brutality rather than the other way around. Like Hezbollah and Hamas, DAESH focuses much of its effort on the populace. They brutally coerce submission and draw their support from select elements of Islam by way of a sophisticated campaign waged in the media and on the ground locally.

The Assad regime in Syria and those elements fighting the regime often utilize the same strategies to maintain control and rally support. It could be well inferred that the current stalemate is as much a part of the population centric strategies of all the entities on the battlefield as it is their access to arms, logistics and will power. All sides in fact see the affected populace as a "tipping point."

Allied/Coalition forces, while employing far more lethal and sophisticated weapons, have struggled mightily because they have little effect on influencing the population. There are significant risks associated with ignoring or poorly engaging affected populations. As an IO (Information Operations) practitioner in combat zones, I have learned some absolute truths these past few years. One is that no matter how much an entity messages something, or how much they spend or invest in HA (Humanitarian Aid), the message must be reinforced and linked to visible actions. DAESH knows and practices this concept exponentially better than does the anti- DAESH Coalition. Appropriate messaging and observable actions are cornerstones of soft power.

DEFINING THE PROBLEM

Irregular Warfare challenges that these days encompasses much of the globe, and some of our most challenging planning also requires integrating foreign governments, agencies, and non-government entities.

The Syrian situation is an example of the effects of applying military capabilities towards the symptoms of conflict rather than the cause of conflict. We and our allies are using nearly exclusively kinetic capabilities to degrade DAESH. While we are decimating their leadership, their ranks are hardly depleted, the human suffering is unabated, and the adverse impacts to the region has grown exponentially. If we had defined killing existing DAESH fighters as the overarching problem to be solved, applying kinetic resources as a primary weapon would be a good step. If, though, DAESH is only part of the defined problem, then by default we are not working towards a comprehensive solution.

As we look at the Levant, is it accurate to "define" our problem as degrading/defeating DAESH? I would suggest that putting the DAESH "genie back in the bottle" only goes part of the way in defining our problem in the Levant. DAESH is but one symptom requiring treatment and that geo-political balance in the Middle East is much closer to a well-defined problem that we can plan/strategize against. Whether we define this as the problem or at least the majority of the problem then by default, kinetic efforts against DAESH also by default take on a secondary role in any strategy to rebalance. DAESH, Hamas, ANF, Khorasan, or Hezbollah by this definition then do not define the problem to be solved but become contributors to the critical imbalance that threatens the Levant and all entities associated with it. Their state sponsors also become part of the problem as they ever increasingly pursue hegemony or strategic parity.

Assuming that balance defines our problem we can start allocating capabilities, both K (kinetic) and NK (non-kinetic) that can contribute to achieving the NSS (National Security Strategy) objective of rebalancing the region.

There are many components to de-radicalization process "turning" recruits. Addressing grievances and mitigating the roots of "piggy-back" causes, will contribute to degrading DAESH, for example, resolving grievances for many of DAESH rank and file fighters like Sunnis being ostracized in Iraq would starve DAESH of a large number of recruits and tacit support. Conversely, applying kinetic effort against those with legitimate and resolvable grievances also would simply perpetuate both grievance and the perception there of. These underlying grievances are very much at the core of rebalancing the region. We in the West tend to see grievance very much as a state issue but in the Levant as in much of the non-western world, the complex layers of grievance are as often between significant players at or far below the State level. Examples of this are Shia/Sunni, water rights throughout the Levant, tribal, economic disparity, and access to markets. Kinetic or "hard power" effort plays little to no role in mitigating any of these grievances. Defining our mission and problem as rebalancing the geo-political balance of power in the Levant will require application of far more NK "tools" than military muscle.

Some Assumptions Going Forward:

- Conflict in the region is directly attributable to both State and Non-State actors vying for either Hegemony or secure equity in the region.
- Much of the conflict is carried out by proxies.
- Human suffering has long ago reached a catastrophic level.
- Most of the entities involved in conflict do not have either the will or the capacity to achieve sustainable stability.
- Sustainable balance will require addressing (not necessarily resolving) all grievances capable of re-triggering violence.
- Continuing instability is a significant threat to the global economy and then by default global stability.
- Significant progress regarding mitigation cannot be achieved by solely applying kinetic tools/capabilities.

- The application of kinetic resources should prioritize targeting individuals, groups and geography that with success will provide access to and opportunity for grievance mediation and relief of human suffering.

OBJECTIVE AND LINES OF EFFORT

We need to focus our Lines of Effort on the three truisms identified by the Joint Operating concept for Irregular Warfare to achieve our objectives.
Here again are the "truisms" regarding irregular warfare:

- Influencing foreign governments and populations is a complex and inherently political activity;
- Irregular warfare is about people, not platforms;
- Waging protracted irregular warfare depends on building global capability and capacity.

Our overall objective should be: *Rebalancing the geo-socio-political issues in the Levant in pursuit of sustainable stability. Rebalancing the geo-socio-political issues in the Levant in pursuit of sustainable stability* as our objective is generalized enough that it should allow a great deal of flexibility in our LOEs and their associated tasks. *A robust and effective communication strategy is organic to and underlies all that follows.*
Lines of Effort (LOE):

- Relieve suffering

  - Legitimacy and credibility will result from mitigating the ongoing and expanding humanitarian crisis created largely by the Syrian Civil War and DAESH. Doing so both reinforces the "high moral ground" approach and mitigates some of the potential for expanding grievances.
  - Humanitarian relief must cut across religion, ethnicity, affiliation, and statehood.
  - Relief also inhibits expansion of conflict areas of operations because once those affected become more secure and by default stable, they become part of the solution rather than the opposite.
  - Relief should be prioritized to meet the most immediate demands of security, food, shelter, water, and medicine.
  - The more humanitarian aid is seen as a collaborative effort, the less ethnic, religious, and state affiliations compound potential delineations that feed grievance.

- Any entity mitigating suffering becomes the "good guy" and draws a stark comparison between themselves and those individuals that are still perpetrating violence against the innocent.

- Diplomacy

    - Diplomacy at the state level is the only mechanism that can begin the truce and resolution process. The UN is seen as impotent and often bearing allegiance to one side or the other.
    - Although diplomacy is "top down" in a region where so many of the most significant challenges are "bottom up" it is still important in managing the impacts/ramifications of state focused agendas.
    - Some of the most complicated and divisive issues are only directed at the state level. For example: access to alliances, ports, oil, trade routes, and sanctions. While these issues are important to state level decision-makers, resolution failure directly impacts both stability and increases suffering to innocents.

- Grievance resolution

    - As previously discussed, there are grievances contributing to instability all the way from the very top (state level) all the way down to the "grass roots."
    - Different mechanisms for grievance hearing and resolution do not exist for all types and levels of grievance resolution.
    - JOINT/Coalition facilitated mediation mechanisms must be facilitated at all levels.
    - The bottom line is that when people talk with each other, they shoot at each other far less often.
    - It is the mediation process that is critical. Expectation management should be applied liberally here. In order to institute any cessation of hostilities, aggrieved parties must communicate. Talking may lead once again to hostilities but the initial mediation at least opens a door of opportunity that cannot be achieved during hostilities

- Kinetic targeting

    - Kinetic targeting must be planned to support three primary items:
    - Leadership, at least three tiers deep in order to degrade command and control, erode morale and interrupt momentum;
    - Destroy and interrupt logistics/support;
    - Provide access for HA and stabilization efforts which deny adversaries terrain and influence over additional persons and support.

- Capacity building

  - Capacity building to continually enhance the strengths and access of Coalition resources that contribute to the first 4 LOEs.
  - We should add more partners, not just states.
  - We should streamline command and control of not only the kinetic effort, but even more importantly, the non-kinetic effort.
  - Evolve and adjust mediation and diplomacy assets as the situations change.

DEVELOPMENT OF THE CONCEPT OF "CUSTOMIZED" SP CAPABILITIES

A capability is a tool to be wielded to help us achieve our objectives. As an Information Operations Officer I had a variety capabilities at my disposal. The traditional capabilities were, PSYOPS, Electronic Warfare, Civil Affairs teams, and Public Affairs teams. These were merely tools to be used in a specific variety of ways to help me influence a target audience. Like most tools, they are not used all the time or even the same time in each application but they are still tools in our tool bag.

Information Operations applied in support of United States Special Operations Command is a custom project. Every mission has its own unique requirements, which in turn require a unique approach, high grade practitioners with specialized, and often non-standard tools. IO involves using a variety of Military Specialists in a variety of capabilities to achieve a custom goal: the ability of a country to persuade others to do what it wants without force or coercion.

IO, in support of conventional warfare, and by doctrine, is much like building the "prototype" construction project. It is focused largely on standardized capabilities, which in a HW (Hybrid Warfare) context do not come close to meeting the complex and challenging needs of strategy. In my tours in Afghanistan operating in the IO realm in support of Special Operations, influence and persuasion were my focus. Learning to adapt and employ non-standard capabilities taught me that there are so many factors on the battlefield that can influence target audiences, not just what doctrine provided. This is precisely the case with soft power.

The geo-socio-political parameters of the Levant are obviously more challenging than a tactical AO (Area of Operations) in Afghanistan. Though bigger and more complex, the concept is the same. We must identify any and all potential "capabilities" that affect or come into contact with our target audiences in order to assess whether or not they are capable of persuading target audiences to align with our National Strategic Objectives. Identification of capabilities outside of what is allowed by doctrine is an art form and not a science.

IDENTIFYING CAPABILITIES

In concept, identification of a potential capability is shockingly easy. Assessing its value and potential role in a SP strategy is the art aspect. As we look at the Levant, let's reconsider Lines of Effort and consider some non-traditional capabilities.

Overall Objective and Supporting LOEs

The overall objective is *Rebalancing the geo-socio-political issues in the Levant in pursuit of sustainable stability.*
Supporting Lines of Effort:

- LOE1: Diplomacy
- LOE2: Relieve Suffering
- LOE3: Grievance Resolution
- LOE4: Capacity Building
- LOE5 Kinetic Targeting

Examples of "Customized" Capabilities in Support of Our LOEs

Let us go through our Supporting LOEs and find examples of soft power capabilities that may support our effort. Again, and as previously stated in Part II, all of the LOEs require support from a comprehensive, robust and proactive Communications Strategy with an overarching core Narrative.

Diplomacy

DOS (Department of State) is already fully engaged in a variety of efforts to resolve the current crisis with Syria and DAESH in the Levant. It is clear that the world, region, and local players are confused as to what the current US strategy is. Clearly articulating a plan/strategy is essential to solidifying support, enabling stability and degrading violence in affected populations. Not knowing who or what will be in charge after the "shooting war" places affected civilians in an extended state of limbo regarding alliances, grievances or in the simplest of terms, who is friend and who is foe.

How do we mitigate the unease within the populace and start paving the way for stability? What non-traditional capabilities can become trusted agents of explanation? How do we improve communications to assist these trusted agents? One easily solved problem is the identification of "trusted" communicators.

Western countries have become overly dependent on the Western style press conference. We assume—incorrectly—that if the Public Affairs Officer stands up and briefs a list of "talking points" that the press will write them down and put them on the newswire and everyone will turn on the TV, look at the phone, listen to the radio, or read a newspaper and be magically informed. But in the rural areas that make up much of western Iraq and large swaths of Syria, news and/or information is better disseminated by "trusted" members of a community. If we want to convey the real progress of diplomatic efforts, we must make the effort to build the network of trusted agents. There were times in my Afghanistan and Iraq deployments that we provided cell phones to trusted agents just so that we could keep them honestly and accurately informed. Reliable communications to keep locals up to date on diplomatic efforts that affect them is important.

A trusted member can be a cleric, a mayor, an elder, and so on. What is important is that news comes to locals by way of someone they trust and trusted entities must be built in layers. The local individual needs someone at the district, county, provincial level, and regional levels. Building this structure of trusted indigenous disseminators of information is essential. The PAO (Public Affairs Officer) can still have a press conference but by building a network of trusted dissemination we would no longer have to depend on the conventional PAO to press model and only *hope* that we reached our audience.

In order to enable and amplify the effects of diplomacy we should have interactive webpages that support better informative communication to local and regional audiences. The interactive capability also would support input up, rather than solely depending on top down communication. There are numerous opportunities to be garnered from such a platform.

Relieve Suffering

There is an extremely long list of NGO engagement supporting the anti DAESH and anti-Assad efforts in the Levant. For example, there are NGOs for refugees, IDPs (internally displaced persons), education, medical care, communications, security, etc. A quick scan of the UNHCR website will also note that the US is by far the largest contributor to the funding stream with no close second.

I'm not suggesting that the US take credit for everything, but that we do "market" more proactively the when, where, how, and why of our and Coalition partners' commitment to the efforts. As that there are affected populations across the spectrum of ethnicities, cultures and religious divisions, a key element of relief is our demonstrable commitment to assist equally, regardless of these factors (this supports credibility and trust).

Any and all engagement of affected populations by NGOs are opportunities to "market" US and Coalition commitment to the relief of suffering. Demonstrative commitment is the most credible of messages. We must mean what we say. Demonstrated commitment to the Center of Gravity influences our CoG. This is precisely what Soft Power is intended to do: positively influence our CoG.

The military contribution to this primarily civilian function is in coordination and logistical support. The CA (Civil Affairs) community has for decades trained and exercised what is known as a CMOC (Civil Military Operations Center) whose task is to coordinate, streamline, and support the application of relief efforts in support of Stability. A CMOC style approach to the areas adjoining non-permissive environments allows for more effective engagement of affected persons, our CoG. Effectively supporting and engaging this COG (Center of Gravity) builds the baseline for developing "allies" rather than creating more disgruntled and potential combatants.

We must also identify any and all persons/entities that come into contact with both the affected populaces and conflict zones because they are potential ambassadors in support of "relieving suffering." There are any number of US and Coalition entities both governance and civilian (outside of the NGO community) that routinely come into contact with influential TAs for example:

- Media, both documented and private
- USAID is long experienced in applying engagement in support of National Strategy and they provide opportunity for many types of Stability engagement
- Assistance programs:
- DOS (Department of State) supports or enables a variety of Assistance programs that are generically focused on stability such as;
- Farm aid
- Engineering support for projects
- Education
- Business development

Stabilizing refugee/IDP a populations living at the edge of conflict zones enables the reverse of the "ink spot" strategy employed with fair success in Afghanistan. "Ink spots" were in the middle of conflict zones and the stabilization/empowerment of affected populaces helped to grow stability outward, stabilization at the edges of conflict zones works in reverse. Stabilizing at the edges is more of a "eating a cookie" plan whereas nibbling away at the edges effectively eventually gains stabilized populations' access back to the heart of the "cookie."

A CMOC "on steroids" is the customized capability that is key to the relieve suffering LOE which accomplishes the following:

- Mitigate suffering
- Build trust and credibility
- Enhance regional stability
- Relieve pressure on the infrastructure of neighboring Coalition States
- Stem the flow of Refugees into the EU
- "Eat the cookie"
- Gain allies rather than create potential future "enemies"
- Shape the effort leading towards more productive grievance resolution

Grievance Resolution

No strategy in pursuit of sustainable stability in the Levant can proceed without both a plan and support for Grievance Resolution. Our most important COGs, the affected populaces at this point are saddled with complex and multiple grievances. All of these populations harbored a variety of grievances even prior to the beginning of the Syrian Civil War and devolving of Iraq due to DAESH.

The importance of supporting this LOE cannot be overstated. While there are and have been some mechanisms in the region for mediating in the past, what is called for now is two-fold. First, we need credible mechanisms for CR (conflict resolution) at the strategic, operational, and tactical level. I say credible because at the Strategic level, CR has long been the purview of the UN. To the informed observer of world events these past few decades, the role of the UN has been undermined by its perceived lack of objectivity, and more importantly, its lack of mechanisms to enforce any resolution. Secondly, we must establish, support and enforce CR mechanisms at the operational and tactical/local level. Relying exclusively on a top down approach will not work.

The Sunni tribes in Western Iraq are a good example of a group whose role in the conflict could have been mitigated with CR between them and Baghdad. Even though Baghdad often said the right words, their actions undermined their credibility. A credible and enforceable mediated solution between the tribes and Baghdad would likely have altered DAESH's landscape and success. So, what is it that we need in place in order to support a comprehensive strategy? As noted above we must provide mechanisms for CR. So what would that look like and how do we go about it?

We should begin with enforceable mediation services in refugee camps. Refugees who are still in the Levant will at some point go home. If we do not start setting the stage for them to air and resolve their grievances prior to their return, the pot will continue to simmer and then inhibit collective large-scale resolutions.

Now that the Iranians are at the table there needs to be a regional mediation mechanism. There is no guarantee that solutions will be formed at this level however, without at least a forum, we will be left to judge intent by words and actions which are in the Middle East often times misleading.

The strategic level is where we can most likely demonstrate some initiative by strengthening, improving, and revamping the UN's mechanisms for mediation. As discussed in the Diplomacy portion, bring local and regional audiences into the mix so that they will see themselves as stakeholders and not being dictated to is essential.

The bottom line to CR/mediation is simple. As long as people or entities are talking they are far less likely to shoot at each other. Peace and stability given half a chance more often than not generates its own momentum. Even the process of establishing appropriate mechanisms is an action visible to combatants and aggrieved parties and will provide a variety of openings to enhance stability. Who or what entity can or will host these mechanisms should, like the LOE of "relieving suffering" be open to who is willing, able and has access.

Capacity Building

CB (capacity building) is often seen solely in terms of a military effort and related to arms, training, and logistics. The paradigm shift we need to see is in development of expanded CA resources, foreign military development, and the survey of infrastructure that is foundational to the interests of our CoGs.

CB should also be part and parcel of National efforts by Coalition partners to wield non-kinetic capabilities in pursuit of their collaborative efforts in support of our strategy. For example, in the above discussion re; LOE2, coordinated engagement of a coalition government—say Jordan—along similar lines would pay dividends. Do they currently have the capacity to support LOE2 effectively? The answer is likely, no. They would, however, show improvement if we assist them in CB in support of their non-kinetic toolbox. The Jordanians would benefit, as would the refugee populaces, were we to employ them to teach/train infrastructure development, election support, education development, etc. They have the language skills, the access and the added benefit of becoming safer with well-developed neighbors.

Many of the tools for CB in support of non-kinetic already exist and could and should be employed in a robust way. There are not enough Special Operations Forces to go around considering the current demand globally so expansion and careful application of forces is a current constraint. This will require significant Force expansion as well as a more complex training plan.

For example:

- US SOF (Special Operations Forces) are already world class trainers of foreign military capabilities:
- FID, IW, UW etc. are the mainstay of an excellent legacy program
- PSYOP Forces are expert in their field regarding coordination and support of non-kinetic strategy e.g. CMOC and influence activities
- DOS and a variety of other US government agencies currently engage globally in support of many of the activities requisite to CB. e.g. Department of Agriculture, Department of Education, Health Services, etc. Again, in order to build foreign capacity, in requisite planks of societal infrastructure it will require enhancing and expanding our own resources to support the current demands.
- Mediation services will require training, support and the capacity to train foreign partners on the nuance of this complex subject.

The bottom line to CB is that the robust type of foreign engagement regarding CB that we did during the Cold War is once again a critical gap in US strategy. During the Cold War we engaged nearly the entire globe for the purpose of Influence in support of US Security objectives. Just because we are now in a Hybrid War environment does not mean we should not be utilizing tried and true methods that achieved a respectable amount of success.

Kinetic Targeting

It is no accident that Kinetic Targeting is the last LOE. As laid out in our Strategy, "killing people and breaking things" is in a supporting role to the non-kinetic. The reasons for this is that Kinetic targeting has but two objectives, albeit important ones.

- Degrade and disrupt adversary leadership (down through the third tier) and logistics
- To provide access into denied areas for the purpose of employing LOEs 1-4

As with any proactive engagement, a tried and true tactic that supports success is "carrot and stick." The outline of this strategy is no different. The Middle East, much like much of the world requires observables to make believers out of both friend and foe. Without the stick—kinetic targeting—LOEs 1-4 are significantly hobbled. The hardcore leadership regardless of adversary is a cornerstone of their success. Replacing leadership is hard, and recurring losses is demoralizing. DAESH for example is not entirely made up of ideologues. Ideologues much like a rabid animal are unredeemable and targeting can only be a positive. Rank and file fighters are motivated by a plethora of other reasons. By eliminating the leadership and chipping away at support through non-kinetics works both ends of the equation. Can we get there from either end unilaterally? I think the current status of the Levant offers a qualified "no."

As for non-traditional capabilities in support of the Kinetic role, I would assert that there are few options. The one thing that can and should be done and which is non-traditional is that amplification of the enormous existing dissent between extremist leaders and factions serves the millennia old tried and true tactic of dividing and conquering. Amplification of issues, such as differences of "who is in charge", competition over logistics, mistreatment of fighters, will only serve to increase the very evident dysfunction within DAESH ranks thereby increasing attrition in DAESH/ Extremist forces.

SOFT POWER CS (COMMUNICATION STRATEGY)

Overview and the importance of Narrative

We now come to the all-important CS (communication strategy) that must be an integral part of any effective strategy. Narrative, as the all-important core of a communication strategy, has been largely ignored in our current conflicts stemming from Extremists usurping Islam for their own selfish, immoral and barbaric reasons. *A failed communication strategy has been, in my opinion, why the US and its Allies are still largely flailing against these evildoers more than any other single reason.* Extremism is about individuals acting on extreme ideas, and despite trillions of dollars, lives, and resources expended we are still nowhere near eroding the "idea" of radical Islam or as I prefer, extremism. The bottom line here is that we must stop clinging to the belief that bombs and bullets are the whole solution and invest as fully in a well-developed comprehensive strategy as we do in the Kinetic effort. Even a comprehensive strategy is potentially less effective without an energetic and properly executed communication strategy.

As I listened with keen interest to the President Obama's Oval Office speech in December, my beliefs regarding communications—or rather effective communications—were confirmed. Ineffective communications are still at the heart of our failings. What I heard as I listened intently was, as recommended in our earlier discussions, a more comprehensive approach but in my opinion, still woefully short of all that is needed. The complexity of the problem is very hard to communicate.

The bottom line here is three-fold. First, in a *beltway* mentality so often out of touch with the reality of the world outside it, the obsession with the bilateral approach of diplomacy and military options are the dominant voices.

Second, Western countries—our primary partners—are still, after centuries of misunderstanding the region, miles from actually "getting" the Middle East and the myriad of complex issues that underlie virtually all of the challenges regarding today's version of the conflict. Third, America and much of the West has developed a near addiction with the "sound-bite" method of news/information delivery. This is a tragic "at odds" methodology that may serve a US/Western re-election campaign or the "bottom line" of a news agency but is an epic fail when communicating the complexities of the multi-dimensional problems regarding effective degradation of extremist activity and state actors maneuvering for power in a part of the world wired 180 degrees apart from the West.

Moving on to the CS (Communication Strategy) portion of a comprehensive strategy, I would like to first point out some of the key elements of a recommended Communication Strategy.

We have identified our overall objective as a *"rebalanced and sustainably stable Levant"* which is achieved by way of 5 specific LOEs (lines of effort) listed below.

Supporting LOEs

- LOE1: Diplomacy
- LOE2: Relieve Suffering
- LOE3: Grievance Resolution
- LOE4: Capacity Building
- LOE5 Kinetic Targeting/ Security

The following is the part of our discussion regarding about how we communicate in support of those 5 LOEs and the *9 critical points* we must address to do this properly/effectively.

1. Narrative, narrative and more narrative!
2. Credibility
3. Relationship of actions/observables to communications
4. Cultural nuance as it pertains to a variety of target audiences
5. Who or what are we talking to?
6. The 5 W's of messaging

   a. Who are we talking to and who is doing the talking?
   b. Why are we messaging?
   c. When do we message?
   d. What is the message?
   e. With what medium(s) do we communicate?

7. Evolving communications to keep up with evolving situations

8. Why sometimes the "right message" is an action and not words
9. The critical need for the currently absent "clearinghouse" for US Communications.

NARRATIVE, NARRATIVE AND MORE NARRATIVE!

Narrative (or rather lack of) is, in my opinion, one of the three most tragically flawed aspects of our (if one actually exists) US Communication strategy followed by social media (collection, analysis and dissemination) and a *whole of Government* information entity/agency.

As an IO Officer, I learned the hard way that any Information Campaign devoid of Strategy, planning, resources and a compelling Narrative was much like the old camp race where runners tie their legs together and race. Yes, you can get to the finish line but you'll work harder, go slower, and likely experience more than one spectacular mishap en-route. In yearly deployments to Afghanistan 2009-2013, I slowly, through trial and error realized increasingly improved results in IO campaigns as my skills with narrative improved. I now have had the good fortune to be acquainted with three extraordinary experts regarding narrative whom can speak professionally about the reasons that Narrative is an imperative and how it works. Dr. Ajit Maan, Dr. Patrick Christian, and Alan Malcher, MA have become invaluable allies and mentors in regard to narrative.

As narrative pertains to our strategy, the bottom line, as noted by Dr. Maan, is simply that we need a compelling narrative (story) to explain the meaning of our intentions and actions. As noted in my opening, the President in his December Oval Office address was trying in a very short period of time to deliver the meaning of how we are or will engage the world regarding ISIS, or as I and many others prefer to call them, DAESH. Additionally, addressing DAESH in a region that is a veritable minefield of complex underlying grievances is even more difficult to explain. Fourteen years into this conflict regarding extremism we still struggle to easily explain just what we are trying to do and why.

Part of the reason that this is so difficult is that the components of clearly viewing our challenges are rife with social, cultural, and geo-political nuances. The same words in English do not necessarily translate well to those speaking different languages in different areas of the world. This is true for both our adversaries and our Allies. Not only do words matter, but so does culture. Another but equally demanding reason for clearly and regularly communicating our narrative is that even for people fully immersed in the DAESH we now face, the issues are so complex that we must make every effort to keep everyone, Allies and adversaries alike, fully understanding our intent and actions.

Storytelling outside the West is often culturally, one of the most important and convincing methods of effective communication. Even in the West, getting a good story onto the *New York Times* bestseller list is also an art form. A good story must stand alone on its own merit. In our case, we must use our narrative much in the same manner as Aesop or Samuel Clemens. We must use our story/narrative to make a point(s) in a manner that will keep the attention of the audience.

So what is the moral of our story? What are the points we must compellingly make? How do we hold onto our audiences? How do we help everyone understand such a complex problem set? These are some of the most important questions in developing our narrative.

Before we wade further into our specific narrative we must know also acknowledge another critical point. Even though we must have an overarching narrative we must also develop multiple supporting narratives that speak to Western, international, regional and local audiences. Dr. Maan calls these interactive narratives and I defer to her expert opinion for further refinement of this concept. Supporting or interactive narratives are all related to the overarching narrative. They tell much the same or very similar story but in a contextually nuanced manner that captures/holds the attention of different but related audiences. The same story and words will not speak the same meaning to different audiences in large part because we live in the West and regional/local indigenous audiences see the world through vastly different eyes. This point demands that the communicator of our narrative by all accounts should be the best culturally attuned messenger. For example, POTUS (President of the United States) may well communicate our Narrative overview to US and Western audiences but someone "on the ground" in Syria or Iraq and at the local level may well be a mayor, tribal chieftain or a SOF (Special Operations Forces) team leader. How do these different messengers make the narrative understood?

For example, the Narrative at the POTUS or Secretary of State level may sound something like the following:

> The US, in pursuit of our own and our friends' security and interests is in a conflict with extremists usurping legitimate Islam as a tool of power. It is not only security that compels us to act but we, as a significant and responsible global partner and acting on our inherent American values have a moral duty to act in defense of the helpless. We realize that these evildoers have nothing to do with Islam nor do their barbaric actions reflect the tenets of Islam. The terrors they inflict on innocents continue to do harm to citizens regardless of faith, ethnicity, culture or region. They are evil and we intend to pursue justice and stability in the interest of all civilized states and their citizens. We intend to continually increase our ongoing support for degrading the immense human suffering, support stability by way of supporting safe mechanisms for hearing grievances, aggressively pursue diplomacy as a key component of grievance

resolution, and, most of all, pursue security by relentlessly targeting all extremist leadership and support of extremist organizations. We do not care where these evildoers hide: we will find them, destroy them and effectively build capacity for all responsible partners that support our efforts. We realize that this effort will not be accomplished quickly or without the pain of financial and human sacrifice. It is, our moral responsibility to act and support all those that share our concerns.

A supporting/ interactive narrative at the regional level might be communicated by forward military commanders, regional diplomats or high profile US citizens coordinating humanitarian aid such as USAID or recognized NGOs. It will by default speak to the narrative spoken by POTUS but be nuanced to "connect" to a regional audience. It may sound something like:

We Americans and Allied partners, along with our regional partners are continually cementing all available regional partnerships in pursuit of eradicating the evil of an extremist and that is attempting to hijack one of the world's great religions for their own evil purposes. Here in the region, we daily see both the grave results of evil as well as the true courage of responsible partners banding together for the eradication of evil and the relief of human suffering. The reasons we support these partnerships is complex but two of the most important reasons are, first, we and the responsible people and states of the region can no longer stand by while evil destroys the lives of innocent people and, secondly, everyone, not just those in the region suffer from the effects of catastrophic instability.

Every day, the partnership between Western and regional partners grows stronger and the physical strength and emotional draw of DAESH weakens. This is always the case when good and decent states and citizens band together against evil. Honorable and decent citizens regardless of race, culture or citizenship are today combining their courageous efforts to once again destroy evil.

We also see that even with the destruction of evil and states that support it that there will be much work to be done in building a stable regional foundation that will prevent further attempts of evildoers to establish a foothold for their selfish interests. We have no illusions that this will be easy.

Part of our combined efforts in building an enduring foundation of stability will be to support any and all responsible mechanisms that provide for hearing and resolving grievances. We also realize that no mechanism will or could ever exist without security. Included in our capacity building much of the focus will be on resources that guarantee security so that the most critical of our goals can be met, which is to mitigate the inestimable human suffering that has been visited upon innocents regardless of religion, culture or Statehood. DAESH, despite their illegitimate claims of statehood has failed at the first requirement of being a state, the care and protection of all its citizens.

Although many of the partners operating here in the region hail from Western cultures, we clearly and irrevocably support our local partners in their undeniably correct assertions regarding the failed attempts of DAESH to represent any legitimate aspect of Islam. We of the West—though not qualified to

argue the religious aspects of Islam—support unflinchingly the qualified condemnations of DAESH by the respected and recognized religious authorities
from around the globe and especially here in the region. Again, no respected
religious authority regardless of Sect, recognizes DAESH as anything but
evildoers usurping Islam for their own selfish and barbaric reasons. These are
not the words of the West but our trusted and respected Muslim partners that
hail from region.

Finally, the eventual and certain outcome of the anti-extremist coalition
will be the destruction of extremist capability, degradation of their evil and
hypocritical ideology, and a stable Levant that has for the first time in decades
a real chance at a bright and prosperous future on the world stage.

These two narrative examples must be supported with interactive narratives at the local level that speaks to each TA (target audience) be it tribal,
local, village or otherwise. The key here is language, cultural nuance and
appropriate trusted communicators. This local level of narrative has tremendous advantages because much of the narrative communication can be accomplished F2F (face to face) by trusted communicators whether SOF (Special Operations Forces), Coalition partners, trusted populace leadership etc.

The bottom line to interactive narrative is that each and every version
must relate to the overarching and be delivered by the right messengers using
the right language(s) and observing the most culturally nuanced approach. As
you can see from the two examples above, both speak in different but supporting manners to the LOEs described in the strategy. They may not say so
in the clearly delineated manner of Western military planning but there is
little doubt as to the meaning.

Finally, in regard to narrative, we must tell our story often, at every level
and with the best culturally nuanced communicator. When notable actions or
events occur, we must repeat a version of our narrative that addresses the
action/ event and clearly articulate why that particular event/action speaks to
our overarching narrative. An important note here is that by way of years of
experience messaging in support of operations, I found that there was no
message that resonated as clearly as one that was connected to a visible
action by the intended TA. For example, it was always much easier to sell
reintegration in Afghanistan after successful targeting of Taliban leadership.
When local Taliban saw demonstrable success against their leadership they
were far more receptive to coming off the battlefield by way of Reintegration
than before their leaders were targeted.

As a brief summary note to the narrative discussion I would like to add
that the bottom line to narrative in a comprehensive strategy is that no one,
ally, foe, or affected populations should be confused about our intent. We
must tell our story, tell it often, tell it to everyone in the most culturally
nuanced way possible, and we must highlight our actions regularly that are
demonstrative of our intent and as communicated in our narrative.

CREDIBILITY

Credibility is the second most essential element to any communication effort after narrative and yet the hardest element to achieve. The bottom line here is that without credibility, no message, no matter how well crafted and executed is worth the effort. Like all messaging efforts, there is no silver bullet. The element that makes a mundane but important message better, or an excellent message priceless is credibility.

I have spent most of the last four decades interacting with folks from the Middle East and South Asia. Whether Christian, Muslim, Jewish, or otherwise, I have learned the importance of pairing messaging with observables.

How could we more effectively message about the successful targeting of second and third tier leaderships in Raqqa? Just like in the narrative discussion, what and how we say something matters depending on the TA. At the strategic/international level saying that "we have killed a certain number of influential DAESH leadership in Ar Raqqa because they are evil-doers and their actions do irreparable harm to all." Would support our overarching narrative. The regional level messaging should say something more along the line of, "we have killed a number of DAESH leaders that have caused immeasurable chaos and destruction to the regions of Syria neighboring Turkey and Iraq which have impeded cooperation by partners in the fight against extremist evil. Eliminating DAESH leadership gives all parties in the region an opportunity to achieve the stability that is beneficial to all save the evil-doers." At the local level, we would have a far better chance of resonating with the local audience if we said something like, "The US/Coalition air-strikes recently witnessed by so many of Ar Raqqa's beleaguered citizens, killed the evil doers that have been killing, torturing and oppressing so many of Raqqa's sons, husbands, wives, and friends for the past four years." The point that counter's the extremist message effectively is that we are not saying we killed Muslims but killed evil doers, in order to protect people of all faiths/sects from the evil of DAESH.

What you can see by the above examples is that the message needs to provide a reason for the TA to connect with the message. I know that when I listen to the six o'clock news, my interest will be heightened if I hear a story that is on a street near where I live or it potentially impacts someone I know. The part of the message that captures the attention of the TA must be an emotional "hook" that makes the message personal to the audience. Truly understanding a TA so that the message and messenger can regularly speak to that emotional hook also builds credibility.

Regularly messaging any TA with reliable information tied to an observable builds credibility. Like the old saying regarding trust though, "it takes a long time to build trust, and only a second to destroy it." The same adage holds true with TAs and messaging. This simply means that we must regularly message in conjunction with observables so that our TA in a region that perceives information differently from us actually starts reliably associating credibility to our messages.

This last point has been a real challenge for the US in the past. We are often so consumed by getting to the actual truth surrounding an observable that the ensuing delay offers the enemy the opportunity to be first in media. Remember, our adversaries also experience observables and in a messaging vacuum by us, they will fill the vacuum with their own message. There is absolutely nothing wrong with prefacing our official statement with, "at this time, this is what we know to be true. If, as things develop that alter our perspective, we will be forthright with the details." We must be first and absolutely as truthful as we know at the moment. Over the course of time, repeated and regularly truthful statements build our credibility and decreases DAESH's even if it means being honest about a mistake.

We learned the lessons of the last paragraph by way of years of experience in Afghanistan. The SOP (standard operating procedure) we developed there proved intrinsically that this system works. Before this SOP was developed, we regularly were subjected to Taliban claims of civilian casualties because they got the first word in the media. The result was a halt to Operations which gave the Taliban a chance to recoup and degraded our credibility with the Afghan populace. Once we started publishing the results of night raids at the crack of dawn and offering "corrections" when we found out otherwise, resonating claims by the Taliban dropped to historic lows. The bottom line here is that by being first and being as honest as possible, we slowly acquired credibility.

The connection between credibility and regularly correlating the "why" of the raid as stated in our narrative also cannot be overlooked. Part of every morning's statements about raids also included the "so what" of the raids. For example, each raid's announcement sounded something like, "last night's raid in Khowst province resulted in the kill/capture of X number of Taliban leaders that have been terrorizing the innocent and decent citizens of Khowst Province." This subtle note regarding the differentiation between Taliban and innocent civilians effectively contributed to eroding the Taliban narrative of occupiers/infidels oppressing Muslim/Afghan citizens.

Finally, a note about honest in building credibility especially when we have been in error. As part of our narrative I believe it to be wise to acknowledge our part in the destabilization of the Levant. For the informed, there is little doubt that the 2003 invasion of Iraq set some of the fallen dominoes in motion. I am in no way suggesting that all that has occurred regarding instability or extremism, *"DAESH style"* is due to US actions. Most folks in the region, regardless of religion, ethnicity, culture, or otherwise believe this to be true as well. There is a saying in IO that "it's always easier to message something that the TA already believes to be true." In this case, we are playing to this perceived truth and in doing so will start to rebuild some of the credibility we have already ceded.

To summarize the key points to this portion of our CS discussion regarding credibility I would highlight 5 key take-aways:

*   Recognize that regional and local TAs are "wired" differently and as often as possible message in conjunction with observables. In fact, let very few actions go unmassaged.
*   Be first with the message post observable and correct as necessary.
*   Be honest even in the face of a challenging or erroneous event.
*   Always message with the "so what" that relates the message in some way to our Strategic, Regional and Local Narratives in order to condition all TAs to our narratives' key elements. This way no TA will ever have to ask "why." Remember, narrative tells the meaning or the "why."
*   Always place the most credible, culturally attuned messenger at the microphone, keypad, or TV monitor.

Observables on the topic of extremism and its impact on multiple TAs (target audiences) occur nearly every day and all across the region. These are opportunities to sustain messaging that supports the LOEs in our strategy and as regularly reinforced by way of our narrative. As this CS (Communication Strategy) is in support of a recommended operational strategy we must link our CS to the 5 recommended LOEs because the CS is correlated to the operational strategy. Following are some examples associating observables to messaging for each of our LOEs.

For easy reference, here are the 5 identified LOEs to our recommended Strategy:

*   LOE1: Diplomacy
*   LOE2: Relieve Suffering
*   LOE3: Grievance Resolution
*   LOE4: Capacity Building
*   LOE5 Kinetic Targeting

LOE 1: Diplomacy

The US, its partners, and even our less than complicit and unofficial "semi allies" like Iran and Russia, are regularly involved in some type of diplomatic effort regarding Syria, Iraq, and the Levant. Although DoS and some media often talk about these efforts and the challenges, we must find a way to amplify the aspects of these efforts that relate to our strategy regarding rebalancing the region. Again, our narrative should be explaining the "why" of these diplomatic actions, but if we do not regularly amplify the tenets of the talks that speak to our strategy then we are allowing the emotional connection between TAs and our narrative to lag. When attention lags, an effort to re-educate must be advanced after a sustained period of non-discussion. The re-education takes time and resources that are better applied to progress rather than a two steps forward and one step back method. One of the most significant downsides to this lag is that the perceptions of those most affected in the region begin to believe they are being left to fend for themselves. This "feeling" of being left alone, erodes the credibility that we discussed in the last topic.

Continued engagement sustains emotional engagement in the TA which, when properly messaged, encourages TAs to engage decision-makers to move towards our objectives. In this case, we must "connect" our messaging/ narrative to our overall objective of "rebalancing the region." A quick note here about rebalancing: I am not talking about the rebalance or sphere of influence discussions in the classic diplomatic sense but merely pursuing the objective of balance in the sense that we achieve a more stable atmosphere in the Levant where state and non-state actors back away from a war footing and the acute fear of activity by those they see as adversaries. In a sense, this definition of rebalancing is a sustainable de-escalation of hostile agendas.

A large part of messaging before, during and after diplomatic activity is to explain in common terms what was intended, what happened, and what to expect next. Diplomatic activities, like every other field has a very specific language that is more often than not misunderstood by people on the outside. Local audiences, especially those experiencing conflict related suffering, want to know, in the most immediate terms how will this impact life today. Will the shooting stop today? Will the aid come to my village today? Was DAESH driven out of the village of my family? Messaging about Diplomatic activities is just like any other type of messaging in that it must relate to a specific TA.

Every diplomatic event has the potential to either give hope or degrade hope in an affected population. As that this is a very emotional issue for those on the sharp end of the conflict related suffering, every effort must be made in order to help all TAs to better understand just what each diplomatic headline means. Some of this understanding must be in the nature of expectation management as typically diplomacy is a very long and protracted affair. Relating messages about achievements and/or hindrances to a diplomatic event must also be tied religiously to our overarching narrative. Remember, narrative tells the "why" of our story. Most assuredly, everyone suffering wants to know why, when will it stop, who is doing what in order to make it stop, and can they expect relative stability any time soon.

LOE 2: Relieve Suffering

Every day in the Levant, the EU and the US there are heroic efforts ongoing that are focused on mitigating the overwhelming humanitarian issues resulting from the sustained conflict in the Levant. The heroes are both government and private and they are providing countless observables every day across the conflict zone. As one of the most important LOEs in our strategy we must focus the attention of those affected on just how much is being done, highlighting the gaps and illustrating just what is going on to address those gaps. If we are to build credibility and stake out the moral high ground requisite to erode the DAESH narrative, then messaging on relief is essential.

Particular interest in messaging at the tactical level should be accomplished in areas where recent targeting of DAESH/extremist leadership has occurred. There are a variety of reasons—some classified. When HA is delivered to previously DAESH dominated areas is a clear sign to both those affected and DAESH that progress is being made and victory is imminent for anti-DAESH fighters.

Messaging success with a picture in a recently reclaimed area also denies DAESH or our adversaries the opportunity to say that they still hold the turf. DAESH may use dishonest graphics, but nothing sells like the truth and it is hard to deny a picture that shows a local power-broker like a Cleric, tribal Elder or Mayor standing in front of an aid pallet in the town square.

LOE 3: Grievance Resolution

For those looking at the ME (Middle East) for more than a couple of years, it is all too apparent that the number of conflicts and grievances are seemingly endless. While we are currently focused on DAESH, Syria, Iraq and the Shia/Sunni divide, these are but a few of the large-scale grievances. There are also things like tribal/cultural/ethnic issues across the region, the Israeli/Palestinian issue, water rights in nearly every country, income inequality, sectarian issues, and geo-political issues like oil and trade.

Every affected community in the Levant is normally saddled with multiple unresolved grievances and is no doubt agitated to the point of action at their lack of ability to have these addressed. The bottom line is that even with a Syrian resolution, the pots will continue simmering as that most of the citizens of the Levant believe that the outside world only cares about what is affecting it at the moment and in their eyes it is likely refugees and terrorism.

It is likely that this LOE is the most difficult to associate to an observable. That does not mean that it should not be high on our list of priorities. Any event such as a budding alliance between anti-DAESH groups or the settlement over road or water access that is achieved by way of mediation should be aggressively marketed and couched in the terms of "grievance resolution" by way of non-violent means. Although this is a tough one, we also must in our strategy orchestrate the building and sustainment of conflict resolution professionals/organizations that facilitate collective resistance. The truth is that there are very few professionals trained and experienced in resolving conflicts grounded in non-Western indigenous populations

LOE 4: Capacity Building

In a long term fight with civilian populaces as a COG (center of gravity) we must find a way to build reliable non-military capacity in affected countries and regions that will be advantageous to empowering a stable populace. In support of this LOE we must consider building capacity for beleaguered and affected countries/ regions across the spectrum of governance. This applies especially to those aspects that affect quality of life issues for the populace. *Extremism may be a virus built on ideology but chaos, grievances, and failed states are the petri dishes that empower a virus to become an epidemic.* There may be no cure or vaccine for this epidemic but we can certainly erode the catastrophic impacts on the populaces that enable anger, fear, and discontent to grow to into extremist violence.

Affected populations looking for a way out of their circumstances are by default limited of hope. If they cannot see or hear prospects for improvement they have little to no choice but to tackle their problems by way of the easiest most accessible means. All too often extremists like DAESH, Hamas, and Hezbollah have used this dynamic to their advantage. That is why the observable and messaging piece of this LOE is of critical importance.

Every day, there are countless acts of aid rendered across the Levant. Those acts provide the observables. These acts, when applicable must be coordinated to build a stable foundation for capacity building. The acts that contribute to basic needs such as security, food, water, and shelter speak to stabilization but what is missing is the so what. It is not enough to just say or suggest we are meeting basic needs but to tie these efforts to the stability requisite to the sustainable capacity of host nations to manage and support their citizens. Education, governance, infrastructure maintenance, and civil structure are all non-military aspects of CB.

Here again, a sub-narrative comes into play as we tie the observables to our narrative in a manner that speaks to the long-term goal. For example:

> This year, in refugee camps around the region the US, Allies, NGOs, partner nations and entities provided education, basic needs, occupational and professional training, classes in governance, and civil structure to affected populations yearning to go home. The intent is two-fold: to help these innocent citizens acquire the knowledge and strength to one day in the near future return home as capable citizens that are better prepared to support and build a stable

state and most importantly and to mitigate the inestimable suffering imposed on these citizens by DAESH and their former oppressive Governments.

While it is our moral responsibility to render aid to the suffering, we also acknowledge that it is everyone's best interest in the long run to achieve stability and with populaces better prepared to support long term stability.

This is but one example of messaging. The point explains why we build capacity towards the goal and ties that is observable for our narrative. When it comes to capacity building and supporting messaging, virtually no act or effort should be without the full support of media, public affairs, and put into context reinforced by Department of State. The bottom line here is to deny our adversaries their interpretation of our actions. It is also important here to note that when local citizens see investment in what comes after, they will start to believe more fervently in seeing a light at the end of the tunnel. This is an emotionally charged advantage not to be overlooked. If we want to empower a populace, few things solidify hope better than visible signs of investment in their future.

LOE5: Kinetic Targeting/Security

Messaging to correlate kinetic activity (kinetic targeting) to our narrative is the one aspect we do fairly well at this juncture. We have had a lot of practice. Still, no successful mission killing DAESH leadership, degrading DAESH infrastructure, and demoralizing DAESH fighters, or extending DAESH hypocrisy should ever go un-reported. We do regularly report on deaths and number of sorties, but the area of messaging the kinetic/security piece that needs refinement and amplification is the why of our kinetic efforts.

The relationship of targeting efforts and associated inroads into DAESH held areas as observables to messaging cannot be oversold. These successes, much like the previously discussed CB become beacons of hope to those affected populations raptly listening for any and all positive news regarding an end to their intensely personal DAESH. These messages must not oversell but accurately portray kinetic successes. This also builds our credibility. There are few things worse for those suffering than to have their hopes dashed by overly zealous expressions of optimism. Success is being made and DAESH (as a military/state) is being diminished, but what matters most to refugees is that they still cannot go home safely.

This is one of the areas that SM (social media) offers enormous advantage. For example, showing the airstrike that decimates DAESH leadership and logistics in a particular village in SM with a short unnoticeable post is invaluable. Pointing out the dishonesty of DAESH when they deny their losses—as they often do—is important as that it erodes the credibility of their successive messaging or posts. Pointing out in posts that they are barely holding on to an area by way of SM also builds morale in DAESH-opposing forces and sways momentum. DAESH fighters and especially leadership thrive on SM and the best way to beat them at their own game in regards to kinetic success is to show a picture or graphic in SM of their losses, infighting (demonstrable by executions in their ranks) and defeats at the hands of local opposition fighters. Destroy their narrative and their morale and you degrade DAESH.

There is an important but uncomfortable note to this topic. The US military and associated USG entities that have the capacity to relate these targeting observables to messaging are relatively meager in comparison to what our adversaries have. The Presidents new TF (task force) is still nascent and by all accounts far less resourced than required.

CULTURAL NUANCE AS IT PERTAINS TO A VARIETY OF TARGET AUDIENCES

It is virtually impossible to emphasize this point enough. Hands down, culturally attuned and delivered messaging has been the US's most significant deficit these past few years, or more specifically in the post 9-11 era. The point of messaging is be understood.

In Syria alone, there are some 22-23 significant ethnic groups with dozens more sub categories. When you consider that with foreign fighters from all over the planet populating the ranks of DAESH and their ilk the subtle differences in culture are daunting. If we add Iraq, Turkey, Iran, and the rest of the complex societies in the region to the mix we have another whole set of problems in making ourselves understood.

The problems we are facing in the region are beyond complex and we are struggling to make ourselves understood by both Allies and adversaries. There is no amount of effort we can afford to spare to effectively communicate about what we are up to and why.

We are in fact making very good progress kinetically against extremists. Sometime in the relatively near future we may even recover all of the turf taken by regional extremists. The question becomes what then? How do we sustain the peace? How do we communicate in support of our stability LOEs? How do we keep the idea of extremism from once again sparking a large-scale conflict? The answer is we cannot do any of these things if we cannot effectively communicate with all pertinent TAs.

THE 5 WS: WHO, WHAT, WHERE, WHEN AND WITH WHAT MEDIUM

Who or What Are We Talking To?

Tailoring a message or series of messages to individuals as opposed to groups that those individuals are aligned with or impacted by are two different things. The message may be similar, but the emotional hooks are often quite different. When messaging rural, tribal centric Sunnis in western Iraq, it may be of critical importance to individualize a message to the members of a tribe or sub-tribe by discussing the strength of numbers required to combat DAESH intrusions into their tribal territory or basic needs such as security, food, shelter, etc. When speaking to the leadership of those tribes that likely have an alliance network with other tribes, the same message about security may be in the form of assisting in acquiring more support at the provincial or state level. Both messages are about security, empowerment and survival but the words and emotional hooks are different.

The same line of thinking applies when messaging at the operational and strategic level. Individual states and their contributing forces and resources have their own unique interests even though they may be committed to a common goal or objective. An example: messages that speak to Turkish involvement/contributions to the anti-DAESH fight are all too different than those that would help explain events to Western EU partners. Much like we discussed in the narrative portion, the intent of the messages may be the same but the messenger, nuance, and influential factors will often differ. These subtle nuances are at the heart of what must be considered each and every time messaging is prepared for execution. I have found in past efforts to execute a sort of mini checklist. The description I use for this checklist albeit simple is not all-inclusive but will most certainly provide at least a 90% solution when considering any effort that involves influence by way of messaging. The next part of our discussion revolves around my mini checklist or as I prefer, the 5Ws of messaging.

The 5 W's of messaging

- Who are we talking to and who is doing the talking?
- Why are we messaging?
- When do we message?
- What is the message?
- With what medium(s) do we communicate?

A CS (communication strategy) is a dimensional effort as opposed to a linear one. Most Westerners are hard-wired to think linear. Military campaigns are also often conceived in linear fashion. This is one reason that IO (information operations) planning does not always mesh well with a military or a national security strategy campaign plan. The bottom line here is that those executing any plan or strategy must give full appreciation to both the Linear and Dimensional aspects of a plan rather than focusing on the type of wiring they may have.

The 5Ws of a CS are about as dimensional as can be. The application of any communication strategy can be executed in nearly as many ways as can be imagined. That is why at this stage of our discussion it is important to see this strategy as a guideline, not a road map. Road maps are linear and usually do not allow us to see or understand the variety of nuances in the topography along the route.

The issue at the forefront of US political discussion right now on Islam and Muslims is a very good example of the *first "W"* (what). There is no doubt that many of our regional TAs sense a "war on Islam." Extremists are very forthright in selling their narrative regarding this cornerstone issue. The hate regularly displayed in the US and Western press towards Muslims also increases the risk of undermining the very Allies we need as our credible messengers to erode the ideology of the extremists. In fact, the shrill tone of Islamophobia, (the what), plays so neatly into the extremist narrative it is almost as if they were in some way orchestrating the cacophony of Western Islamophobia. Our narrative is the vehicle for explaining the sometimes sub-tle but critical differences in fighting DAESH, but not Islam, we must make every effort to employ our narrative or salient parts of it far more regularly (the when), with surgical precision and deprive Islamists of this windfall of propaganda. This point alone justifies regularly explaining, by way of our Narrative, *what* we're really up to and *why*. Again, I cannot emphasis enough that everything we message must in some fashion be tied to our overarching narrative.

Another item on the *"when"* list is any and all instances that highlight the hypocrisy of DAESH and their fighters. Evidence of rampant hypocrisy is regularly visible online and in SM but the ability of the US and its partners to expeditiously *(when)* turn these instances into a valuable influence weapon and amplify them appropriately does not currently exist. We need the ability, along with regional partners, to analyze and disseminate in a manner that does the most good. This includes technical tools within SM (Social Media) that help to identify the most appropriate material. *(Social Media is an example of "with what medium")* We also must have the best analytical tools available that will not only identify the material but also analyze the most effective dissemination paths (connectivity analysis) that enhances the viral potential of our messaging. Klout scores, connectivity analysis and network analysis are just three of a variety of technical applications needed but not yet effectively employed.

Wrapping DAESH and their minions of foreign fighters in shame due to evil and hypocritical behaviors *(what)* is a well-established tactic for influencing behavior of recruits, potential recruits and fighters *(who)* that are already disenfranchised. Shame that is conferred on recruits by SM publically "outs" fighters to their families and support networks at home for evil and un-Islamic behavior. Shaming (again, shaming is the *"what"* of our actions) when coupled with degradation of morale due to leadership decimated by kinetic means is a powerful combination of punches to the gut of DAESH.

Ideology is both DAESH's strength and its vulnerability. Every day, respected clerics *(who)* across the Sectarian spectrum of Islam condemn DAESH fighters and actions as un-Islamic. Sadly, Western Media does nearly nothing to improve the dissemination of these invaluable condemnations. When we talk about degrading online recruitment, it is my belief that robust, regular *(when)* and nuanced amplification of the condemnations by respected clerics in Global Media would pay measureable dividends in diminishing recruitment *(why)*.

It is important here to note that these condemnations and refutations are most effective if they cross sectarian and regional lines. In other words, it may be good for a Jordanian Sunni cleric *(who)* to issue a Fatwa *(what)* against DAESH but if he does so with a Sufi, Shia and other Sunnis regardless of Fiqh (School of Jurisprudence) then the impact is far more effective and unifying.

The current polarization of US politics does a great deal of harm to this important effort. Considering our most significant vulnerability in the States and Western Europe comes from home-grown terror plots it would seem like a "no brainer" for both sides to go "all in" with this support but somehow the point is lost on most media. Homegrown terrorists *(who)* are difficult to identify therefore even harder to influence. However, if the news online is full of counter-DAESH condemnation by credible voices from within Islam *(who)* we have a far better chance of the right message finding its way to the vulnerable regardless of whether it is initiated as part of a cohesive strategy *(why)*. It's not about control and who gets credit for discouraging recruitment. We also may never know who or what had the proper impact but at least, by encouraging and supporting amplification we increase our chances of success. No contribution should be ignored.

I would also recommend altering language around "martyred" persons as seen in Jihadist postings and replacing it with language that confers no honor such as saying "so and so was killed before he could commit another evil and heinous atrocity" (the why). It is also recommended that a summary of barbaric acts attributed to these leaders is part of the story as a way to delegitimize and dishonor them. This is even more important for Western fighters because the attached shame of being a terrorist diminishes the call to honor in prospective recruits (the why). As with the discussion above under the head-ing of culture, each and every community foreign fighters hail from have their own nuanced view of honor and shame. A campaign I used to great effect in Afghanistan played on organic Pashtun concepts related to honor and shame. These cultural overtones are powerful influence tools and behavioral modification messages. Evolving communications need to keep up with evolving situations and the critical need for the currently absent "clearinghouse" for US communication.

Communications of the complexity that we are discussing here require a C2 (command and control) structure that enables rapid and effective communications to meet those changes. The USG does not at this time own the capacity to C2 messaging. There has been a food fight of sorts for years within the USG over types of messages, message primacy, release authority, legal authorities, and so on. Like all bureaucracies, these battles are often about budget, hierarchy, and even finally about content.

The problem as an IO Officer at the tactical level is getting messaging approved that would impact things at the strategic level had no less than ten levels of approval authority. I was involved in daily operations did not have the ability to rapidly message to local TAs in the immediate aftermath of an event that had Strategic implications. There were work-arounds but there was no way to speak with the authority in support of the USG. These ten or so levels were only in the military chain of command but there are also numerous different levels of agencies and entities of the USG outside the military.

As we can see from recent events, for example, such as Turkey shooting down a Russian aircraft, an event can have strategic implications very quickly. We all know here in the US that old news is irrelevant. When there is so much on the line as there is almost daily or even hourly in the Levant, we can hardly afford to be irrelevant. Sure, it's great that DoS or CENTCOM can speak from an officially sanctioned podium but how does that help everyone below that level? Like politics, the most important influence is often local.

Communications in today's day and age operate in "real time" Benghazi is an example of why we need not only messaging capability to impact/influence events and TAs but also to provide analysis in real-time as to what is going on. This requires a variety of SM tools common to marketers but far less so in the USG. For example, real time monitoring/analysis on the ground can tell us what is going on, real time analysis can tell us what it means and what can or should be said. It then can help us disseminate through the most connected paths to the most important TAs and then finally, there are tools that can help us reassess, analyze and adjust a message for effectiveness according to a changing environment on the ground.

This capability, in order to be effective, would have to exist in an OC (operational center) so that all relevant decision-makers would have access to information and be able to make real time decisions about responses. The OC would also have to have the ability to develop and coordinate dissemination of follow-on strategic communications and all other types of communication required to support our CS on a daily basis. Right now a small amount of what we described sits in the State Department, COCOM (Combatant Command) Headquarters, regional commands, country teams, etc. These entities, whether across the street or half way around the world from each other, are so disjointed that it makes for a version of the game telephone. By the time messaging is coordinated it is either so distorted or is overcome by other events.

In the aftermath of 9/11 we built, staffed and operate NCTC (the National Counter Terrorism Center) that fuses intelligence capabilities from the disparate elements of the IC (Intelligence Community). This is a fairly good model for what can and should be done in the communication world of the USG. The non-kinetic application of power is the key to winning America's emerging and present conflicts in the coming decades. This begs the question, why do we not have an entity to manage the myriad of components that make up the non-kinetic, of which information is a key element?

The key to mitigating adversarial influence in Afghanistan after a kinetic event or in day-to-day support for our overall strategy was to own the information space. We did not get this right all of the time but when we did, it demonstrated beyond challenge the power of well-orchestrated *Information Operations*. Considering that in the Levant we currently have far more kinetic events than boots on the ground either mitigate adversarial influence or exploit a success without a greatly streamlined C2 structure for communications. Kinetic, as we discussed in the Strategy portion is but one of 5 LOEs (lines of effort). Although less exciting than the kinetic, the non-kinetic has far more to with eroding extremism and its underlying grievances than the kinetic. Unless we develop and support a C2 communications structure that has the capability to operate at the speed of modern events we run the risk of being irrelevant in all 5 LOEs.

CONCLUSION

Here is where we come full circle in a communication strategy. If we agree that DAESH is a movement and a movement requires as much non-kinetic effort as does the kinetic then by default, we must not run the risk of being irrelevant by failing to communicate effectively about what we are doing and why. This is a monumental effort to be sure, but again, we no longer have any choice but to get busy.

The bottom line is that we must start regularly communicating effectively about our intent and degrading the "brand" of our adversaries, be it extremist or those they are aligned with. We must either recreate an agency to harness and execute our strategy or dramatically streamline the C2 between the myriad of players involved in our strategy. Talking about it and/or using a think tank strategy is not an option at this point. We are in crisis mode whether we like it or not. If we get this effort "right," the system or tool will be available for any DAESH we meet in the coming years and decades. The hard lesson of our countless irregular warfare challenges is that influence is every bit as important as a tank or an F-16.

Chapter Two

Syria-Iraq

Beyond the Zero-Sum Narratives

Amar Cheema

"After much occasion to consider the folly and mischiefs of a state of warfare, and the little or no advantage obtained even by those nations who have conducted it with the most success, I have been apt to think that there has never been, nor ever will be, any such thing as a good war, or a bad peace."—Benjamin Franklin

GENERAL

Strategic interests are often made out as compelling reasons for nations to go to war. However, what lies behind most (national) war agenda(s) are opportunities created by a select few to profit and plunder. "Those who make war do so for many reasons, although many of these are never acknowledged publically."[1] In this world of socio-economic imperfections,[2] exploitation of man over man has been and remains a societal normal. It is the familiar lust for power and greed that drives the war in what was once the bountiful land of Mesopotamia.

Within the conundrum of this regional conflict, also lies the raison-de-être of the ill-defined and broad-based (global) war against and/or of terror? When viewed with a wider backdrop—the global geo-strategic setting—it is evident that not only are the two inter-related, but inter-twined: sub-sects of the larger game played for retaining/re-gaining control. The US and a resurgent Russian Federation seem to be playing the familiar great (zero-sum) game; an imperialist throwback of the last century. The stakes of this latest power play are larger than any regional victory. For the US, it is for maintaining its global primacy, and for Russia, it is for regaining a modicum of strategic balance. Be that as it may, the unfortunate part is that the ancient land of Syria and Iraq—the cradle of mankind remains a land ravaged by war, conflict and exploitation; energy resources— the elixir of the modern world has only added to its woes.

THE CONTEXT: IRAQ-SYRIA AND THE GREATER MIDDLE EAST

While America has been carrying on a systematic and sustained campaign for keeping the region unsettled and in a state of perpetual war, Russia too is all in. Beyond Syria (and Ukraine), Russia is involved in a price war of crude oil—a war that could impact its strategic progression. Paradoxically, in this, its interests converge with that of the US, since, after gaining self-sufficiency, America too is under pressure from its energy industry to break the stranglehold of the price war calibrated by/through the cabal that controls the Organization of Petroleum Exporting Countries (OPEC). The dynamics of this dog eat dog game are yet another dimension that fuels the flames in the greater Middle East.

It is also important to highlight that things have not being going right in the ongoing war against terror. Despite the use of high-tech weapons and sophisticated surveillance means against what are portrayed as irregular forces there have been no real gains. Despite the successes, the adversary's power base not only remains secure but is visibly stronger. Judging by the rising costs of Homeland Security, and the siege mentality that has shrouded the world, it would seem that terror is winning. Despite the US led global war on terrorism (GWOT), the cult of fundamentalism, and incidences of terror used as a weapon, have not only increased but escalated in terms of their frequency and intensity. Repeated attacks—in and beyond the region— downing of a Russian jetliner over Egypt and subsequently of military aircraft by Turkey and its sponsored groups, and the continuing Iran-Saudi (Shia-Sunni) feud, has taken this conflict to a higher level.

Judging from the number of actors that are involved—within and out of the immediate battle zone—it would also not be incorrect to view this conflict as a world war. The scope is definitely global and principal powers of the world are involved, albeit, with divergent aims and objectives, and limited means.

For the world caught in another spiral of hatred and violence, it is prudent for mankind to think beyond the traditional zero-sum narratives, and in this context the earthly wisdom of Albert Einstein, the visionary-scientist of yesteryears, is pertinent to recall: "We cannot solve our problems with the same thinking we used when we created them." The world also needs to take a cue from the words of the political activist, Karl Marx who changed the history of Czarist Russia: "Philosophers have tried to explain the world, our task (now) is to change it." The aim, therefore, is to think beyond the self-created morass and aspire for a future beyond the current logjam created by extra-regional actors.

Taking the campaign to its logical conclusion is the collective need of the hour, and just as the world came together in the two great wars, the time to act against a common threat before it gets out of hand has come yet again. Despite the myriad interests, this multi-cornered contest can still be made as an opportunity in the larger interests of humanity. However, unless and until this happens, this global war—a war that affects entire mankind—is unlikely to succeed.

CONFLICT RESOLUTION:
APPLICATION OF HARD AND SOFT POWER

Just like war and peace are perceived to be extremes in the conflict spectrum, soft power (SF) and hard power (HP) may appear to be on opposite sides. In practice there are multiple overlapping layers in the vast shadow area that exists between them: their application and/or integration limited only by imagination. Being mutually inclusive and inter-dependent, convergence of HP and SP application is required not only in terms of the aims, but also in the collective progression of do-able strategic and operational objectives.

For practitioners of HP and SP, the important point about this unequal war that effects entire mankind is that of victory, which does not translate as the destruction of the adversary. More than physical destruction per se, it is about the negation of the idea of terror and its use by man against his own kind. Thus, apart from being a kinetic war that requires HP to make tactical gains and to shape/ ensure the ends, the larger (strategic) aim requires constant focus on the War of Ideas. Making and sustaining perceptions is more important in this war than obliterating targets and therefore focused application of do-able narratives to build and then sustain the peace is the key.

Since terror is a potent and ever growing threat, there can be no debate on the use of HP to take it out. However, beyond the application of force, the campaign needs to be taken beyond to ensure an effective eco-system for ensuring collaborate security. The aim therefore, must be on achieving long-term goals: tangible results that are lasting and self-sustaining. Since HP and SP have their own domains (both in terms of time and space) their application needs to be synergized, sequenced, and choreographed in concert with each other. The bottom line is that they need to support as also supplement each other. In the ultimate analysis: "power being the ability to affect others to get the outcome one wants."[3] In this case, the outcome that is desired is the end of what essentially is a regime of terror and return of peace—both in and out of the region.

WEST ASIA: ARENA OF GREAT POWER GAMES

The war raging in west Asia, especially in Syria and Iraq, is not only transnational but also multi-faceted. Its effects go well beyond the region. At the internal level, it is a civil war, a secessionist war, and for those who are not directly affected, it is a repulsive Sectarian bloodbath—a throwback to medieval times. At another plane, it is a high voltage proxy war being waged between the US led western world on one side and the Russian led Troika of Iran, Syria, and Yemen on the other. At yet another level, it is made out as a civilizational war between the Christian world and a medieval Arab world. However, at the regional level it is more of an internecine feud between Sunni/Salafists versus the others, including the other sects of Islam: a blood fest that started centuries back and seems destined to continue in perpetuity.

While all these are in some way justified, the bottom line is that firstly, beyond the smoke-screen(s) and subterfuge, this is a war being waged over energy resources and control over its lucrative trade: pillage and/or its denial being the agenda. Secondly, this is a war for retaining/gaining strategic control over the real estate linking not only the eastern and western worlds, but providing a gateway to the Eurasian landmass and the fissiparous underbelly of Russia.

In his seminal book, *The Grand Chessboard: American Primacy and Its Geo-Strategic Imperatives* ,[4] Zbigniew Brzezinski, the former American National Security Advisor, outlined his grand strategy for leveraging the regions strategic location and for doing so, exploit the inherent volatility of the Middle East to pries the Eurasian Balkans open. This would not only provide the US, the key to the riches of Central Asia, but at the same time would consolidate its hold over the energy sources of west Asia. It was this strategic direction that led to the wars in Iraq and Afghanistan, which not only resulted in the marginalities of Iran but also in eliminating the monolithic Soviet Union as a strategic competitor to the US.

In 2007, Condoleezza Rice who succeeded Brzezinski after a hiatus of two decades took this initiative forward and outlined an even more aggressive blueprint for an Anglo-American-Israeli initiative. This envisaged the creation of an arc of instability extending from Lebanon, Palestine, Syria, Turkey, Jordan, Iraq, Iran, and through Pakistan extending to Afghanistan. Advocating a grand strategy of divide and control, this set the stage for unleashing what has been termed as constructive chaos. And to a great extent, it is the chaos that has been engineered thus far, through promotion of terror outfits and by providing material support to both state and non-state actors that has torn the region apart.

The US, on behalf of the free (sic) people of the world and its allies, initiated a Global War encasing on the emotional upsurge of 9/11. At that stage, President George Bush, Junior declared, "our war on terror will not end until every terrorist group of global reach has been found, stopped and defeated."[5] However, despite the prolonged engagement in Afghanistan and the regime changes in Iraq and Libya and even the mayhem in Iraq and Syria, this has still not happened. Conversely and perhaps, in keeping with the aim of the so-called constructive chaos, it was not designed to happen.

Having said that, it is a reality of the times that the Al-Qaeda and its affiliates continue to flourish. In an indirect manner have spawned the Islamic State of Iraq and the Levant (ISIL), or better called the DAESH, an acronym for the Arabic phrase al-Dawla al-Islamiya al-Iraq al-Sham. It is the collective threat that they now pose across the globe that has become a clear and dangerous threat for mankind. At the same time, it needs to be underscored that for the select few who drive strategy and dictate policy that: "war is not only a profitable business but also an enticing elixir" – it is this thinking that essentially benefits extra-regional actors that keeps the conflict going.

Coming to the situation at hand. While the regime change in Iraq and Libya provided shallow tactical victories, the war was/ is by no means over – Syria still stands between the Persian Gulf and the Mediterranean Sea, though, President Bashar Assad's regime remains under tremendous pressure by the DAESH, and the numerous moderate (sponsored) terror groups who between them had/have a single point agenda: take control of Syria. By doing so, ease Russia out of the region in strategic terms. The ultimatum issued recently by the US for transition of power in Syria makes their intent clear.[6]

It was under such circumstances that Russia was constrained to intervene to prevent Damascus from being run over. Not only was/is Syria a valuable Russian strategic ally, it cannot be ignored that the Mediterranean Coast provides Russia an invaluable foothold outside mainland Russia. The maritime base of Tartus and the air base at Latika, the key to keep its sea lines between the Black and the Mediterranean Seas open.

On his part, President Putin is also proving an important point: resurgent Russia is back in the strategic calculus. The match may have been lost in the late eighties, but the game was still on. Russia is thus playing for larger stakes than Syria per se and along with Ukraine, this seems to be where she has drawn a line. This realization seems to have dawned in Washington, but despite the significant success on ground, no change has been evident in the US regional/global strategy thus far.

In baser (economic) terms, this war is not merely over control of energy resources—especially over the pipelines and waterways that conduit this vital resource. More importantly, it is about the economics connected to this trade, and ipso-facto, it is about the longevity of the (imbalanced) petro-dollar global economy. This throws up another question: would the world continue with the US dollar based economy or would there be a switch to a basket of currencies? To an extent, it is expected that the outcome of this war may also redefine this paradigm, making retaining status quo a highly desired outcome for the US.

Beyond the immediate horizon, low hanging fruit in terms of short-term gains are expected to be worth well over $150 billion. This windfall is expected within the next decade, gains for which would be disproportionately in favor of the western world. For the interim, it remains boom time for the arms industry, as war is great for business and a sustained war requiring an endless supply of arms and munitions is even better. Either way, it seems to be a win-win situation for the west, the moot question being what would be the tipping point: the overrunning of Europe in cultural and demographic terms or another episode like 9/11?

TERROR: A PARADIGM OF MODERN TIMES

As defined by Wikipedia, the word terror is derived from the French word *terrorisme*, which has its origin in the state terrorism practiced by the French government in the years 1793-1794. As it has currently come to be understood, terrorism relates to the killing of innocent people for political purposes; its modern use going back to Sergey Nechayev, who founded the Russian group Peoples Retribution in 1869, and who described himself as a terrorist.

Though there is no universally acceptable definition of terrorism—the why of it being a matter of interpretation—a UN report of 2004 describes this as any act intended to cause death or serious bodily harm to civilians or noncombatants with the purpose of intimidating a population or compelling a government or an international organization to do or abstain from doing any act. Over the past few decades, terrorism has become a powerful tool to effect political violence and the asymmetrical conflict that is being waged in west Asia is expressly designed to maximize terror and generate psychic fear. Terrorism exploits the media in a big way to gain exponential publicity to impact the targeted audience(s) in order to attain its political goals and/or end states. The inability to counter this phenomenon is therefore a collective failure of the modern world.

TERRORISTS ARE WINNING THIS WAR!

Terror has struck the heart of the free world repeatedly and fear has forced nations to enforce stringent preventive measures: Europe is witnessing unprecedented racial violence spurred by the influx of refugees in large numbers. It is evident that terror is succeeding and therefore winning the war of ideas as the broader aim of terrorism entraps the free world in a self-imposed siege. At the same time goading the world into escalating the war, terrorists seem be attaining their aim to take the war across the world and by so doing, extending the (virtual) reach of their Caliphate.

Paradoxically, rather than narrowing differences, the information revolution that has connected the world seamlessly has also accentuated the differences by beaming graphic disparities between the haves and have-nots. It is ironic that the medium of speech, press, and cyber space—all symbols of the free world—are being exploited by these merchants of death in a skillful manner to win the ideation war. Use of social media both to shock the world and also to enlist bloodthirsty converts to their ranks, has become a principal weapon in the arsenal of terrorists. As posted in the Washington Post: "The dual messages [videos put on the social media] are designed to influence a divided audience. The beheading, immolations and other spectacles are employed both to menace Western adversaries and to appeal to disenfranchised Muslim males weighing a leap into the Islamic fray."[7]

This skillfully choreographed propaganda campaign seems to be succeeding as more than 30,000 foreign fighters from more than 115 countries have flooded Syria since the start of the civil war.[8] In a report, Swati Sharma goes on to highlight that amongst this flood of foreign fighters, at least 4,000 have come from Western countries.[9] These statistics suggest that the campaign is succeeding. The west may think they are be playing hardball, but the Jihadis seem to be playing Jujutzu: the Japanese Martial Art that leverages the opponents strength against itself.

SCOPE

Though the specter of terror spreads worldwide and across many fronts, the focus of this chapter is on the unrest in the ancient land of Mesopotamia. It is over this resource rich and strategic landscape that connects energy starved Europe with Asia—and as described by Robert Kaplan in geo-strategic terms—as the shatter zone for the landmass of Eurasia,[10] that power games fuelling the conflict are being played. The intent is clear: divide and conquer. By so doing, capitalize on the gains that accrue. The US and Russia engaged in most—in some places with boots on the ground—others by supporting operations in an admix of hard and soft power application.

Despite the pall of gloom and little hope on the horizon, the perspective offered here is of an eternal optimist: the aim being to suggest do-able themes and present narratives that recommend exploitation of both HP as well as SP, prosecuted to their logical conclusion. At the same time the concerns of India both as a regional neighbor and an actor that has the potential to broker peace with willing participation of the affected powers has been presented. In this war where there are many conflict(s) of interests and may seem improbable. However, hope is the essence of life and a world at peace with itself, a celebration for mankind. The earlier the world realizes that gains from such nihilistic pursuits are self-defeating, the better for mankind.

The paper is structured in three parts. First, (Building) Divergence to Convergence, followed by Application of HP and SP for Winning (the interim) Peace, followed by recommendations for Sustaining Peace.

FROM DIVERGENCE TO CONVERGENCE

Before attempting to build consensus on the end state for a region as turbulent as West Asia, it would be useful to highlight the purported aims of the principal actors, as convergence is only possible if aims are matched against each other. At the same time, despite the differences, both US and Russia realize that escalation of the confrontation—especially if it becomes direct and if it necessitates boots on the ground—is neither desirable nor affordable. In view of this given the necessary mediation and consensus of sorts is therefore possible. At the same time, there are some areas where convergence is still possible provided peace is recognized as the common objective. In order to do so, certain imperatives are highlighted to understand the differing stands, which on the face may appear to be inviolable. Hence may be moderated and/or relegated in priority, in favor of the do-able options.

Perceived US Aims and Objectives

From the American perspective, creating and maintaining a state of instability in this strategic region was—and in the views of some hawks in Washington may still be—desirable. In keeping with the publicized US strategy of divide and control, a settled Turkey, Syria, Iraq, Lebanon, Iran, and even Israel are not conducive to national interests: peace would not only preclude positioning of US led forces in the region, it would also undermine the raison-de-être for it to maintain over-arching control over the strategic gateways of west Asia.

At the same time, it is increasingly being realized in Washington that this strategy of sustaining chaos may have been an option for the US of the eighties and nineties. However, after the recession and the costly wars in Afghanistan and Iraq, there is a realization that American power is on the decline: a reality with which the US must reconcile and recalibrate strategic objectives. At the same time, energy security, which was the principal driver for US control over the energy rich countries, is no longer the same strategic compulsion. After the Shale Revolution, the US has not only become the largest producer of crude oil and gas but has emerged as an exporter.

This leads to another issue of crude oil pricing. OPEC, primarily led by Saudi Arabia, has been waging a price war in the past few years, which has taken a heavy toll on the US and Russian energy economy. Logically, both would desire to break the OPEC stranglehold. Though this has its own complicated dynamics, consensus in some form or the other is possible on this and connected issues.

Within these changed imperatives, a settled Iraq and resolution of the prickly issue of Kurdistan and capping of Iran's nuclear ambitions could be additional areas where convergence can be generated. If this is acceptable, the destruction of the DAESH and Al Qaeda could be viewed with a different perspective. This would still leave Syria and other parts of the troubled Levant out of the immediate ambit. Israel, both as an effected party and an American ally also has a lot at stake and needs to be an active partner in building peace in the region. However, it has its own agenda to destabilize Turkey, Syria, and Iran. In manner Israel is furthering its agenda is apparent from its support of Kurdistan. At the same time, Turkey—which has played an underhand role all along—has been exposed as the principal spoiler: a role that Pakistan had played in USs war in Afghanistan. Turkey therefore needs to be restrained in along with the traditional (Sunni) spoilers of the region, Saudi Arabia, Qatar and the like, who have their own interests and agenda for fuelling the conflict.

Russia's Aims and Objectives

Irrespective of the (purported) common US-Russian aim of targeting the face of terror (Al Qaida and DAESH), there is neither commonality of intent nor in the operational methodology. From its perspective, Russia needs to muscle its way back to great power status and for a foothold in Syria. Maintaining a strategic signature in the region is its paramount. Andrei Tsygankor[11] opines that "Putin's long standing objective has been to establish Russia as a nation that acts in accordance with formal and informal norms of traditional great power politics and is recognized as a major state by the outside state." Thus, even though Russia has withdrawn the bulk of its forces, its military presence is expected to continue. In addition, Russia needs to navigate around the crude oil price war and to counter the impact of natural gas planned to be piped from the region to Europe at the cost of Russian supplies. These are tricky questions that have no straightforward answer. If some common ground is to be found, it must be part of a larger strategic arrangement brokered between Russia and the US.

Do We Have Convergence?

Convergence could still be built around the immediate areas of interests: for the US it is Iraq; for Russia it is Syria. Indirectly, both have reasons to cap the regional aspirations of Turkey, Saudi Arabia and Iran. If both agree to keep their immediate operational focus on their respective areas of interest, lines of operations could be worked out. Still, the prickly issue of Kurdistan—which effects Iraq and Turkey more than it does to Syria—needs attention of the US, with support of Turkey and Iran who are the other affected parties. Under the circumstances, this seems complex and difficult, but must be made an agenda for the future.

A UNITED APPROACH TO COMBAT TERROR

By definition, terror is the ability to instill intense fear. Anyone who exploits fear by whatever means is a terrorist. Without getting into the endless debate of who created whom, the reality is that locals are terrorized by violence unleashed by both state and non-state actors (non-state actors/forces being anathema for any society). At the same time, they are caught between the proxy wars between big powers. Which terror is greater is a matter of perception. If the war on terror is to have any stabilizing effect, it is this fundamental perception that has to undergo a change. This is a salient issue around the world and Arab world and the Indian Prime Minister has stated this in no uncertain terms.[12] There cannot be a good or bad terrorist be it the DAESH, Al Qaeda, Taliban, LeT, JeM or the like: a terrorist is a terrorist. Anyone who commits a violent act of terror must be branded as a criminal. The bottomline being that support of terror outfits must stop. No longer can the world afford to draw a distinction between good and bad terrorists: a terrorist was and remains a universal threat for civilization. The day this is universally clear, the better for mankind.

Winning Peace

The timeless wisdom of the ancient strategist Sun Tzu merits recapitalization: "the acme of warfare is to defeat the enemy without fighting." While hard (command or kinetic) power is indispensible in any war—be it in application or for projecting a threat to prevent conflict or its escalation—the application of soft (co-optive) power is many times more potent and lasting for building and sustaining peace. Smart power combines the elements of HP and SP in mutually reinforcing ways. Seen in the light of the advice of Sun Tzu, prevailing over the adversary should (ideally) be leveraged through the medium(s) of SP through the propagation of ideas and by so doing for moderating and changing perceptions. If possible this should be supplemented by HP only when necessary with the means and quantum dictated by the operational situation and the desired end state. Notwithstanding, the ends and means need to be well thought through and must be appropriate to the threat(s).

The world also cannot ignore a lesson from history recounted by Henry Kissinger in his paper published in 1969 after America's ignominious defeat in Vietnam. "We fought a military war, our opponents fought a political one. We sought physical attrition, our opponents aimed for our psychological exhaustion. In the process, we lost sight of the cardinal maxims of guerrilla warfare: the guerrilla wins if he does not lose. The conventional army loses if it does not win." Going by the trajectory of the war in Iraq and Syria, it seems that history is being repeated. Kinetic means may be able to obliterate physical entities of terror, but they cannot kill the idea, which requires application of smart power. SP application, through all possible means, is the need of the hour.

In terms of conflict avoidance and for shaping the immediate battle space, the application of SP before, during and after physical combat is paramount and indispensable for success. Application of such power is required to be in accordance with the desired end state. All tools directed towards meeting the end, and must be exploited concurrently. At the same time, peace building requires an all-pervading conviction that peace can prevail. There is a requirement for building synergy in action, and in order to do that, a requirement to determine the nature of the adversary and environment. By so doing, decide on the target groups for application of Kinetic as well as SP individually and collectively.

In order to manage peace and shape the battle space, the full spectrum of resources and mediums to project SP must be exploited intelligently to attain the aim and or to generate the conditions so as to make the operational task easier in terms of time, effort, and resources. This has to be done in accordance with a well thought out strategy; and as cautioned by Sun Tzu "tactics without strategy is the noise before defeat." The world simply cannot afford to invite defeat by putting up a disjointed front in this war against terror. There is too much at stake for mankind at large.

WHO IS THE REAL TARGET: ISLAM OR THE TERROR GROUPS?

It is important to highlight that the target of the campaign needs to be the terrorist and the mushrooming cult of terror worldwide. It is not Islam. When viewed objectively, any branding as Islamic terror is intrinsically a flawed construct. As Karl Marx has philosophically said, "God is the same everywhere."[13] As the bottom-line, it would be highly inappropriate to use a term like Islamic fundamentalism as it needs to be understood Islam as a religion has nothing with the propagation of terror. It should also be highlighted that terrorists who kill on the name of Islam only constitute a miniscule minority of the 1.6 billion Muslims worldwide. The vast majority of Muslims do not espouse any regime of terror and for them, Islam is a religion of peace. In this connection, it would be pertinent to highlight that over a thousand Islamic clergymen from India, including the heads of the better known mosques signed a petition (a fatwa) that not only do they do not endorse terror but they also denounce the DAESH and the likes as being un-Islamic. [14] Similarly, despite being a pre-dominantly Muslim state, Indonesia, and to an extent, Bangladesh, have been coming down hard on the outfits who employ terror as a means to further their cause.

At the same time, there is a disconnect in the way the west thinks about religion and its influence on human life. For the western world, as should be the case for secular India, religion is essentially a personal affair and therefore should not be part of political life. Conversely, for Muslims Islam is an all-pervading way of life and transcends all actions. This fundamental difference in the thinking and citizen discourse must be kept in mind by the war strategists.

At the same time, it is also important to highlight that religious fundamentalism is a loosely defined term, especially because of the indiscriminate usage by the media. It is also pertinent to highlight fundamentalism differs from orthodoxy, which implies following tenets of any religious dictates. On a higher scale is communalism, which implies exploitation of religion for narrow but religion based goals. Fundamentalism differs from both by aiming for political goals. Thus, while being a devout Muslim may simply mean being deeply religious or orthodox, it is the exploitation of religion for political (not spiritual) aims that mark the difference between communalism or fundamentalism: this distinction is important to understand for any practitioner of SP in this campaign.

At the same time, it needs reiteration that the term Islamic terror was and remains a convenient creation of the western media. The right or wrong of branding can be debated while the very coining of this term highlighting a threat from the Islamic belt, (thereby justifying western intervention) is wrong intrinsically and remains the nub of the question. At the same time, it is also true fact that terrorism in any form aims to terrorize and create fear. Under universal law, anyone who uses such means towards achieving his/her goals, whatever they be and whatever be his/her physical or religious identity, must be branded as a terrorist.

When and wherever violence is propagated on the name of religion and used as a means for coercion, it needs to be branded as religious fundamentalism. To illustrate, while the LTTE enforced its beliefs by unleashing violence in Sri Lanka, in no way could this be dubbed as fundamentalism. The 9/11 New York bombing of the Twin Towers may be dubbed as fundamentalism, though this too is debatable. Defacing Muslim women as retribution for not wearing the veil and suchlike acts perpetuated on the name of religion need to be universally vilified as fundamentalism. Asgar Ali Engineer, [15] who is considered an authority on the subject, explains, while the act of the Al

Qaeda to bring down the Twin Towers was undoubtedly an act of terror, it cannot be dubbed Islamic Terror. He justifies by saying, "there is no Priest-hood or Church in Islam, who's Fatwa, however eminent the Institution issu-ing the Fatwa is, is binding on any Muslim." He further elaborates, "The religion practiced by masses of Muslims is more spiritual than the politics and religion practiced by the likes of Osama, which is more political than spiritual."

It merits attention that Islamic fundamentalism was—and to a large extent remains—a reactionary phenomenon thriving on a deep-rooted sense of in-justice and on the victimhood of Islam. The sense of exploitation is difficult to shake off and shades are visible even in secular India. Terror groups feed on the sense of deprivation of the downtrodden, which is a result of socio-economic exploitation and the culpability of their leaders over the years. At the operational level, it capitalizes on the corrupting influences of western values, especially of the liberal education on the youth, and on the other hand, eulogizes the virtues of Islam, especially of the puritan Salafi sect. Over time this has created angst and has become radicalized by the conflu-ence of deprivations and hope offered by faith, however gory may be the path and however long be the journey.

Until grass-root problems are addressed, terror will always find willing recruits to fill in the ranks. Becoming a fighter on behalf of the faith is a natural progression for youth for whom neither employment opportunities exist nor are the societal atmospherics suitable for self-employment. It is this unfortunate reality that has to be remedied by socio-economic means and for concurrently rejuvenating social harmony. This is only possible by ensuring good governance: political stability and providing support to the leadership therefore, has to be made priority one. It might also be pertinent to mention that the regime change experiments in Iraq and subsequently in Libya are precisely the change that needs to be avoided: change for the sake of change cannot be an answer. To make a difference, change is required to open up a world of socio-economic uplifting for the people. This should be the central point of all SP campaigns, both to bring about genuine change, and more importantly, to weaken the widespread perception that outside powers, with active connivance of their own rulers are exploiting the people.

THE HYBRID REQUIREMENTS OF THE WAR

The war being waged in the region is a blend of conventional and irregular warfare. Though all sides are applying kinetic force, it is the success in changing perceptions of the people that would eventually make or mar the campaign.

Apart from targeting and population control measures, there is a requirement to wage an economic war on terror outfits across the board. There is also a requirement to apply pressure on sponsors like Saudi Arabia, Turkey, and Qatar to stop their funding of terror. While stopping and/or freezing the flow of funds is comparatively easy (provided the collective will is generated), the difficult part is to stop extortions and fund collection. India had a similar problem in Kashmir and peace could only be restored after enforcing population control measures.

Peace can only be restored by planting boots on the ground, supported by a wide range of humanitarian and psychological operations. At the same time, it is also a fact that fighting a manpower intensive irregular war is anathema for the west and Russia. On the other hand, there seems to be no other way around. Perhaps there is a serious requirement to consider a UN sponsored peacekeeping force supported by a multi-national robust peace building campaign similar to the Marshal Plan for war-torn Europe that followed WWII.

Winning a hybrid war necessitates the use of disruptive weapons, tools, and strategy. The theory of bombing bastions of terror to take out top tiers of leadership has already been found to be wanting. In fact, the specter of terror has grown exponentially. At the same time, the DAESH, Al Qaeda, and the like are not monolithic entities but amorphous organizations that thrive on, breed, and remain among the people. Thus, if and when the war has to be won, it is the people-militant connection that needs to be severed. The strategy of divide and control can be applied effectively by creating dissension between the people and terror groups, and concurrently to turn the groups against themselves; this requires the skillful use of all elements of HP and SP. A recommended theoretical model, employing both mediums for building peace is illustrated in figure 2.1.

Announcing an increase of Special Forces for employment in Iraq and Syria with the task of taking out the leadership signals the US continues to support Iraq. At the same time, it is important to highlight that this may be another case of too little, too late. Precision engagement is the need of the hour, it must be with the specific aim to clear and control the area. Such control should be progressively expanded outwardly, concurrently consolidating in the cleared area. It is pertinent to bring out that despite the major successes evident after the American surge of 2007, US allowed operational control to slip back in the hands of the adversary. It is therefore important that the gains made this time must be consolidated on ground. In the similar way this applies to Syria, where Russia must take the lead.

OPTIONS FOR BUILDING PEACE

Aim: to Restore Politco-Social-Economic Normalcy

Hard Power Options	Soft Power Options
1 Military options, including an UN sponsored Peace Keeping Mission deployed on grid basis 2 Selective targeting of key leaders, including offering prize money on their heads 3 Turkey, Saudi Arabia, Qatar, and Iran are constrained to withdraw their forces and material support 4 Economic sanctions on any country supporting terror outlets 5 Freeze any accounts linked to the terror trail(s)	1 Expose support being provided by key sponsors of terror throughout mulitple means 2 Neutralize/mitigate fundamental media messages by credibel counter narratives 3 Re-establishemnet of necessary services and ensuring normalcy of public life 4 Rehabilitation of livelihood by porviding employment and means for constructive self-employment 5 Schooling of children to be ensured through inducements and allurements

Figure 2.1.

Managing Perceptions

Labeling a good and/or bad war is a matter of building perceptions and traditionally big powers have proved to be past masters of labeling their own wars as just. Fighting against Hitler's Germany, fascist Italy, or even waging an atomic war against Japan were convenient labels to rally support and to maintain the momentum to attain the strategic goals. Similarly, the infructuous war to keep melting pots in turmoil was/is part of the creeping invasion by the US in Eastern Europe. The destabilization of Iraq and Syria is an attempt to keep Iran marginalized and is aimed to prevent it from becoming a regional challenger for Israel, the House of Saud, and the Emirates of the Gulf. There is a requirement to build global consensus and manage the conflict within mutually acceptable limits.

Managing perceptions directed to win the war, and aimed towards building a better future require intelligent application of smart power, firstly, to counter the hold of the DAESH and Al Qaeda over the locals, and secondly, for generating an outrage against the atrocities to justify application of force in the eyes of the local people.

Amongst others, the target population should be the sea of refugees with the aim of turning them against the people who forced them out of their homes. The other target audience would be the people who have braved it out by staying on. This is easier said than done, as within the refugees are embedded sympathizers and even militants, and therefore selection has to be done judiciously. For meaningful success, desire to do something must come from within the refugees and howsoever heartless it may sound, all refugees must not be given refuge in Europe or elsewhere. On the contrary, they must be supported to win back their lives in their homeland: this may be a more humane thing to do in the long run. At the same time, the outrage against the refugee influx in Europe must also be moderated. While criminals must be treated as such, refugees desperate for peace must be provided help to regain a sense of security. Unfortunately, this is not evident, and it may trigger a backlash, which needs to be avoided.

What builds perceptions? In today's world of instant reporting, there is the requirement of being able to discern and focus on the humanitarian work being done and also on the destabilization being done by the adversary: the former simpler than the latter, as incidents are often false flagged and stage managed. The irony of GWOT and even humanitarian assistance being ex-tended is that while emphasis is ensured on the latter, very little, if anything, is done to generate peace for the sake of maintaining peace. Whatever is done seems to ferment further unrest. If that is the aim, then it appears to be successful when deceit and distrust make the soil barren, peace cannot hope to germinate.

The challenge is in making the people who yearn for peace to become receptive to peace building initiatives and to prepare them in psychological terms to purge the venom injected into society. This requires a well-thought out campaign; the moot question is if the free world and the dictators control-ling the region are ready for a soul-searching solution? It is important to highlight taking out toxity after decades of bitterness entails a revisit.

Recreating Credibility

The US seems to have lost credibility in the perception of the locals and is seen as the instigator of the problem and the driver of the conflict. On the other hand, the Russian intervention is seen as an attempt to stand up for its friends. The US, unfortunately, is not. As a world leader, America therefore needs to burnish its image with the people of the war-torn region and also with the rest of the world.

Fundamentally, there are three dimensions of credibility: trustworthiness, competence, and goodwill. The competence of the US and or Russia is not in question but the trustworthiness and goodwill of the US is. This necessitates a paradigm shift in the thinking of the US if she has to regain moral ascen-dency, and by so doing, sustain its global primacy. The message to be sent out has to be clear, unambiguous, and unequivocal: the world stands for fairness and equal opportunity. Mistakes may have taken place in the past, but for the future the US and Russia, supported by the rest of the world, need to undertake the following:

1. Invoke the willing participation of sympathetic Muslims to carry their message. This has to be undertaken at multiple levels, permeating to the grass roots.
2. Develop a well-thought out campaign to negate/ nullify the perception campaign waged by terror outfits.
3. Involve the refugees and victims and empower them to stand up to terror. It is crucial to make them feel that they are not the problem, and the fact that only they can be the solution to their problems.
4. Involve regional partners to mediate in the peace building and keeping.

To answer the basic question if the application of soft power mitigate or deter war, is a resounding yes, but the intent to make it so must be sustained. The truth is simple that the world simply cannot afford to fail. Europe and the US are already reeling against the onslaught, and if left unchecked and uncontrolled, Iran, Turkey, Israel, Russia, China, and India will be the next targets, as would be the Middle East North African countries. It is important to recapitulate that seven decades back, despite the differences, the world had got together in WWII to fight what was then considered a collective threat to humanity. While the success is evident, what was a greater victory for mankind was the rebuilding of the lives and rehabilitation of the people of war torn Germany, Italy, and Japan by collective endeavors. Such an effort is required to be replicated once again in the larger interests of mankind.

SUSTAINING PEACE

Imperatives for Peace

Peace does not simply mean the absence of violence; it is the cessation of war and mitigating/minimizing the reasons that lead to it. For the people who are directly impacted, this means safety, stability, and normalcy in their daily lives. This therefore translates not only to the restoration of public services, but sustaining of the socio-economic atmosphere where one can get livelihood, education etc. without fear or violence. The population, therefore are the center of gravity and the focus for SP application.

Cessation of the War

The world community is seeking ways and means to enforce the cease-fire. All parties directly or indirectly impacted by the conflict must be made part of the initiative, and ipso-facto understand the concerns of the other sides. More than the cease-fire, it is important to get a commitment that sponsoring of terror in in the form of material or economic support is no longer acceptable. It is understood that achieving the cease-fire declaration presents the challenge in maintaining it. This will not only require carrying through of HP options, but to ensure maintenance of the peace. More importantly, these should help shape an environment that would make keeping of the peace indispensible.

It is important to reiterate that all campaigns based on SP requires convergence of aims of the sponsors and support of the local administration to further the common cause, and to take them to their logical conclusion. If there is any dilution on the part of even one of the contributing organization, positive results for this delicate campaign will be difficult to achieve.

Since the aim in this phase is also to prevent potential insurgents from taking to arms, efforts must ensure to keep the affected population fruitfully

SOFT POWER OPTIONS FOR SUSTAINING PEACE

Aims:
1 Continue to restore normalcy in the afffected and immediate region
2 sustain friendly media eulogizing the humanitarian work and support

Specific Measures
1 Ensuring employment/relief—skill development and employment programs
2 Sponsoring higher education for deserving students aimed to keep them away from negativity
3 Schooling of children to be sustainedn through inducements and allurements
4 Involve locals in welfare and rehabilitation measures—empowering local bodies
5 Negate fundamental influences and concurrently promote universality and humanitarianism

Sustained re-education of the affected people and changes in the education system is the key results should not be expected in years, but will take decades

Figure 2.2.

engaged. This is a delicate task and needs to be directed by a multi-national core peace team, and such a team must aim to bring about a self-realization in the population that their lives are stable again. Such a team was created for the rebuilding of war torn Germany and Japan. The broad directions for this phase of the campaign are illustrated in the following figure. India as a large and affected neighbor can not only contribute but with the help of other partners, also be in a position to make a difference in a common pursuit of peace.

Recommended Themes

Skill Development and Self-Employment

Skill development and self-employment are methods of self-help to re-establish lives and livelihood. However, promotion of skill development in order to ensure employment can become a means. This needs to be ensured with the help of regional partners.

Sponsoring Higher Education

Higher education is another step to keep youth engaged. Sponsoring their education abroad, especially in neutral countries would not only help keep them insulated from the negativity of the conflict, but also from getting infected by local influences.

Schooling of Children

Re-establishment of schools would be a big step in ensuring normalcy in society. It should be ensured that children are brought to the schools and an institutional mechanism needs to be ensured to do so. People see their future in their children, and if this group can be weaned away from a life of violence and hate, it would be a major success. At the same time, this is a tall order and requires a sustained and well-executed campaign.

Ensuring the Involvement of Locals in Welfare and Rehabilitation Measures

In the final analysis, the locals must be encouraged to help themselves. This can only be possible through promoting and pushing welfare and rehabilitation schemes, sponsored, and where possible, monitored by the international community. All such endeavors must appear to come from within, as outside agencies are invariably viewed to have their own vested interests.

Negate Fundamentalism and Promote Universality and Humanitarianism

Negating fundamentalism and promoting humanitarianism may sound difficult and even utopian, but in practical terms it could be the simplest. Humans
recognize the intent and can see through the motives. If such measures and
messages can be supplemented by the right messages and body language, it
would provide a positive suggestive influence to change perceptions. However, it needs to be ensured that all such messages are conveyed in a subtle
manner, and wherever possible, through the people themselves. As long as
basic amenities like health, sanitation, supplies, primary child care, etc. are
seen to be extended in a humane and neutral manner, the results would be out
of proportion to the efforts put in.

Winning the Hearts and Minds

Winning the hearts and minds (WHAM) of the people is the ultimate aim of
any counter-insurgency operation, and is the single most important purpose
of the SP campaign. The success of such a campaign may take time and
effort and is frustrating because success cannot be easily gauged. WHAM
lays "emphasis on population support, based on inherent ardor and prefer-
ences, stressing on inner grievances over external influences and laying
stress on economic deprivation and inequality; and on conception of insur-
gent conflict in terms of electoral analogy, where the outcomes are driven by
and reflect the prevailing affiliations of majorities or substantial majorities."[16] In the ultimate analysis, WHAM aims to restore the sense of security, honor and dignity to the individual, his/her family and to the society he/
she lives in. The individual and his/her legitimate aspirations, therefore lie at
the core of the campaign.

WHAM is not an episodic response and can only succeed if backed by a
well thought out and sustained campaign. It is a win-win strategy but requires
focused energy and stability. This is important to understand for two fundamental reasons:

1. Frequent changes and shifting focus is always counterproductive; in-
   complete, or unsustainable efforts frustrates the target population and
   tends to alienate the very people who are supposed to be won over.
2. Perceptions change slowly and therefore, only sustained efforts can
   bring about meaningful transformation.

The aim of application of these SP campaigns is more psychological
rather than physical, though both go hand-in-hand.

> It is a mistaken notion that attainment of security is solely a function of
> military action alone. There is no arguing that military forces have a major role

in counter-insurgency, but they have their own limitations. Where progress has been achieved, it is largely attributable largely to political and economic factors than military ones. Asymmetrical challenges demand asymmetrical responses— political, economic, cultural, informational and psychological tools, tactics and techniques that work over time, not by military forces whose true purpose is to fight and win wars.[17]

Taking the cue again from Sun Tzu, success in such a campaign lies in the success of winning the perception battle and in weaning those who are sitting on the fence. In the ultimate analysis, success in this battle will be crucial to sustain peace in a volatile region as West Asia. "In the long run, winning the War on Terror means winning the Battle of Ideas."[18]

CONCLUSION

In a situation as complex as what is prevailing in the region, aspiring for peace—especially when there is neither clarity nor is there a perceptible desire for peace—may appear to be overly optimistic. If the threat is not recognized for what it is and for what it could portend, the world may witness an era of greater instability. Europe who is bracing an unprecedented migrant onslaught is an example of things that could come.

The major powers need to take a step back and recalibrated their strategies as there is more to gain from peace than from war and violence. At the same time, nations like China and India have the capability and a lot to lose due to the instability have an unique opportunity to contribute to the greater cause of world peace and bring about moderation and stability.

At the same time, while peace building may be the immediate and even attainable objective, it must be ensured that this is lasting. Measures to sustain the peace therefore must be well thought through and put in place. This is the challenge and requires sustained efforts on the part of the world community and more than anything else: perseverance.

Terror has no place in a civilized world and at the same time, linking religion with terror is blasphemy of human values and should be anathema for any civilized society. At the same time, denigrating Jihad, which is a puritan concept of inner cleansing and sublimation of the soul and mind, must be seen beyond this mindless bloodletting. In in its purest sense, Jihad means engaging in the conflict within, and not in inflicting violence on others: the Jihad perpetuated is not only unsanctioned by Islam, but unholy by any book and religion.

Idealists dream of a world without wars, and it is important to underscore the fact that eventually its all about human life. It is about the civilized conduct of human beings, irrespective of religion, caste, creed, or color. If that is disregarded for short-term gains, despite centuries of human civilization, the alternative is a void. That is not the future that we want for our future generations. Reiterating the thoughts of Benjamin Franklins quoted at the start—there is nothing like a Good War or Bad Peace; what has been going on in West Asia is a manifestation of both. The world needs to understand this basic tenet and the earlier there is consensus on this account, the better it would be for human progression.

NOTES

1. Chris Hedges, *War is a Force that Gives Us Meaning* (New York: Anchor Books, 2003), 168

2. A report filed by Mr. Steven Rosenfeld on 19 January, 2016 quoted OQFAM, an international confederation of 17 organizations and working in approximate 94 countries for poverty alleviation that has put out alarming statistics. This states that the cumulative wealth of the top 62 billionaires of the world equals to the total wealth of 3.6 billion people (more than half of the 7.4 Billion of the worlds population). What is even more alarming is the fact that that the gap is increasing: the rich are getting richer while the poor are getting poorer.

3. Joseph A Nye, *The Future of Power* (New York: PublicAffairs, 2011)

4. Chris Hedges, *War is a Force that Gives Us Meaning* (New York: Anchor Books, 2003), 168

5. George Bush Jr, President of the United States, Address to the Joint Session of Congress, 20 September, 2001

6. As reported in the Associate Press, on 3 May, 2016, US Secretary of Defence John Kerry at a Press Conference openly warned that Syrias government and its backers in Moscow and Tehran that they face an August deadline for starting a political transition to move President Bashar Assad out, or they risk the consequences of a new US approach toward the war.

7. Greg Miller and Soued Mekhemmet, "Inside the Surreal World of the Islamic States Propaganda Machine," *The Washington Post*, 20 November, 2015.

8. Ibid.

9. Swati Sharma, "Map: how the flow of foreign fighters to Iraq and Syria has surged since October," *The Washington Post*, 27 January, 2015.

10. Robert Kaplan, *The Revenge of Geography* (New York: Random House, 2013).

11. Andrei Tsyganlor is a Professor at the Department of Political Science and International relations at the San Francisco State University and teaches Russian/post-Soviet, comparative and international politics. He has published widely in western and Russian academia and is the author of *Russia's foreign Policy: Change and Continuity in National Identity* (Roosman and Littlefield, 2006) and *Whose World Order? Russias Perception of American Ideas after the Cold War* (University of Notre Dame Press, 2004)

12. Speech of Indian Prime Minister Narendra Modi to Indian diaspora in Malaysia, 22 November, 2015. This was reiterated by the Indian Foreign Minister in her address to the Arab League. It was to the credit of the League that they not only concurred, but also called for developing a strategy to eliminate its sources and extremism, including its funding. *Hindustan Times* Report 25 January, 2016.

13. Leo Tolstoy, *War and Peace* (New York: Vintage, 2008).

14. More than 1,000 Muslim clerics in India ratified a 1,100 page edict that condemns DAESH and calls extremist groups actions "un-Islamic." Religious leaders across mosques, education institutions, and civic groups across India signed the fatwa, affirming that the actions of DAESH are against the tenets of Islam. The edict was issued by a leading Mumbai-based cleric, Mohammed Manzar Hasan Ashrafi Misbahi, and was signed by the leaders of all the main mosques in India. "Islam does not allow the killing of even an animal. What the DAESH is doing is damaging to Islam." *Arab News*, 23 November, 2015.

15. Engineer is a Human Rights Activist, and heads the Institute of Islamic Studies, and Centre for Studies of Society and Secularism, Mumbai. He has authored 44 books on issues like Islam and communal and ethnic problems in India and South Asia.

16. Brigadier (Ret.) Rahul K Bhonsle, Indian Army, quoting Michael Fitzsman, Nathan Leweiter, and Charles Wolf, "Hard Hearts and Open Minds? Governance, Identity and Intellectual Foundations of CI Strategy," *Journal of Strategic Studies*, Vol 31, No3, 345, June 2008, Manekshaw paper, No 14, 2009, WHAM : Lessons from J & K, Centre for Land Warfare, New Delhi.

17. Col. Harpreet Singh, Indian Army, "Defining Victory: The Dilemma in Anti-Terrorist and Counter Insurgency," *Indian Bureaucracy.*

18. Dr. Antulio J Echevarria II, *Wars of Ideas and the War of Ideas* (Stratecig Studies Institute, 2008).

Chapter Three

Kingdom of Consciousness

Peace-Building Meta-Narratives

Eirini Patsea

SCENE I: THEY WERE THE CHRISTIANS AND THEN . . . THE MUSLIMS

For Faith

And now, as wickeder things advance more fruitfully, and abandoned manners creep on day by day, those abominable shrines of an impious assembly are maturing themselves throughout the whole world. Assuredly this confederacy ought to be rooted out and execrated. Nor concerning these things, would intelligent report speak of things so great and various, and requiring to be prefaced by an apology, unless truth were at the bottom of it. I hear that they adore the head of an ass, that basest of creatures, consecrated by I know not what silly persuasion, a worthy and appropriate religion for such manners . . .

Now the story about the initiation of young novices is as much to be detested, as it is well known. An infant covered over with meal, that it may deceive the unwary, is placed before him who is to be stained with their rites: this infant is slain by the young pupil, who has been urged on as if to harmless blows on the surface of the meal, with dark and secret wounds. Thirstily—O horror! They lick up its blood; eagerly they divide its limbs. By this victim they are pledged together; with this consciousness of wickedness they are covenanted to mutual silence. . . . I know not whether these things are false. Certainly suspicion is applicable to secret and nocturnal rites; and he who explains their ceremonies by reference to a man punished by extreme suffering for his wickedness, and to the deadly wood of the cross, appropriates fitting altars for reprobate and wicked men, that they may worship what they deserve . . . [1]

ie many of this kind—of how early Christians
:mporary fellow citizens in Rome. These narra-
rimination and hostility towards the early Chris-
same time fueled the thirst of the Christians to die
sisted their core identity: in order to make a loud
ght less of them. For when one becomes a martyr

For Freedom

On the Greek revolution against the Ottoman Empire, the suicide missions of Greek national heroes, and the western press.

During the liberation war, it was common that Greek fighters would go on a boat loaded with dynamite, alone, amidst the Turkish fleet, and blow themselves up. These events were portrayed in the western newspapers as unlawful, unjustified, and brutal acts of terror against the legitimate ruler of the region. Now these people are heroes of the Greek nation, honored, remembered by name, and sung in traditional songs: songs that are being taught to toddlers in every school in Greece. The anniversary of the then-unlawful revolt against the legitimate power, the Ottomans, is now celebrated and recognized by all states. These people are not terrorists anymore but freedom fighters and martyrs that sacrificed their lives in the name of the nation, in the name of orthodoxy and in the name of the motherland (in this exact order of significance).

For Faith, Freedom or Evil

The Hadith, Bukhari (52:54): the words of Muhammad, "I would love to be martyred in Allah's cause, and then get resurrected and then get martyred, and then get resurrected again and then get martyred, and then get resurrected and then get martyred."

When we are talking about radical Islamic groups, how can we possibly distinguish between terrorism or martyrdom? These labels refer to the same behavior, framed differently based on perspective: "One person's terrorist act is another's freedom fighting. In the end, the commission of the ultimate sacrifice for one's ideology is the subject under examination."[2] In this ultimate subjectivity, the historical narrative that will be constructed decades from now largely depends on the small political narratives of today: as narratives have the fundamental, extraordinary power to shape reality.

Current war narratives or terrorist narratives or peace narratives for that matter, follow a trajectory of "emotional progression in order to be persuasive; they must resonate with prototypical/archetypical themes."[3] Leaders, heads of governments, heads of armies, and leaders of terrorist groups alike, in times of crisis use an "existing vocabulary of emotion to enable an audience to assimilate events to familiar patterns"[4] and martyrdom for the faith and the nation, for the family, for one's dignity and freedom, is not a strange concept in the war narratives and the peace narratives alike; for through war peace has always been achieved.

Martyrdom generally has the same effect in societies for centuries, "when people see other people dying for a cause, they assume that this cause must be important and must be worthy."[5] A core aspect of this mobilizing narrative is also the reward for the sacrifice that is indeed socially normative. Many of the compensations of martyrdom are social as well as heavenly and the message communicated is ear-splitting.

A relevant theory in the study of radical Islamic martyrdom is that of grievance/threat. This theory recognizes the perspective of the martyrs. It generally emphasizes that those committing terrorist attacks have a different framing of their actions. The behavior is framed as freedom fighting rather that malevolent and unprovoked attacks western society generally believes.[6] Many individuals in these groups believe that they are fighting for a righteous cause against the immoral, tyrannical force of western powers.[7] [8] When the intent appears as righteous, then the terrorists are instantly transformed to martyrs.

Since relativity is salient in the game of international politics, in order to build a successful peace-promoting counter-narrative, one must start with the presumption that terrorists could be indeed martyrs; otherwise, building a bridge in this chasm we created for ourselves would never be possible.

Therefore, we just have to take a step back and try to see the big picture. It is different when one focuses exclusively on what terrorists such as DAESH doing on the ground in this particular moment, than to go back in history and see all variables at play that led to this very particular moment. Is DAESH merely a plague upon humanity or a necessary evil to transit to the next era in history? One is certain, that groups of this kind are never created in a vacuum. They exist because they were created by a successful transcendental narrative, they expand because then they created a successful transcendental narrative for themselves and because the others—the civilized west—have been intentionally stripped away in the name of secularization by the transcendental archetypes that have been and always will build successful narratives.

SCENE II: THE INEXORABLE LAWS OF HISTORICAL DESTINY

A Nation for the Personae Non Grata

The narratives can usually be split in two categories. There are national narratives (how we see ourselves) opposed to reflexive narratives (how we see others).[9] More often than not, a narrative comprises both aspects, such as the below story. In the exact same way, western narratives do the same when telling the story of the inherently violent orient, the west of true democracy and the people living in both.

> Once upon a time, in a land far far away, there was war and then foreign rule and then war again and then foreign rule and then war, civil war, terrorism and then it was emptiness. People fled desperate to find a new home, as what they thought as home does not exist anymore, it is simply a black hole. The people crossed a dangerous sea to reach an island of hope. The island where, as travelers say, a temple lies. The temple of the GOD without eyes. The legend has it that because he cannot see gives sanctuary to all. All. But they were wrong. Gods do not have a voice to talk to this earth and for the priests of the GOD know best, before they even saw the refugees, they declared them "personae non grata." Because they know best. And then there was war on the island of hope.

Let There Be War

Narratives such as the above show how dangerous the attempt to polarize identities could be when forcing people to retreat to conservatism and defense thereby depriving them of the cathartic chance to reflect upon themselves, their constructed surroundings, and their responsibility. A responsibility that is not humanitarian but rather political, is to include the responsibility of the citizens as well as of the states: the principle of *state continuity* permeates the vast majority of modern states' constitutions.

A core aspect of such narratives is also the close proximity they try to imitate with the historical accounts. However, in our days, when historical pressure no longer allows any escape, "how can man tolerate the catastrophes and horrors of history from collective deportations and massacres to atomic bombings if beyond them he can glimpse no sign, no trans-historical meaning"[10] Eliade asks; "if they are only the blind play of economic, social, or political forces, or, even worse, only the result of the "liberties" that a minority takes and exercises directly on the stage of universal history?" It is not possible to accept them without a meta-historical meaning.

The oriental narratives, on the contrary, are rather a "resistance to history, a revolt against historical time, an attempt to restore this historical time, freighted as it is with human experience, to a place in the time that is cosmic, cyclical, and infinite."[11] The myth of the eternal repetition, the quintessence of the abolition of time is what makes strong influential narratives of war and peace. While the orient is using transcendental narratives for revolt, liberation, peace, or even terrorism, the west is trying to talk sense through its counter-narratives. In fact, trying to talk false sense. For bringing emotional and spiritual intelligence in these narratives, many think, equals becoming prey to irrationality and darkness.

However, when the west is constructing war narratives, the transcendental instincts of fear, survival, and combating wickedness are always evoked. What is the difference between the war on evil and the war against the infidels? Why will we not use rationality in our war narratives? A war for gaining control of natural resources sounds *fair* enough to me. It is part of the game that is been played since the War of Troy. It is part of the human nature and a means to satisfy human needs. However, this narrative would not have been enough to mobilize soldiers or tax payers, the same way it was not enough to mobilize the audience of Homer. The question is: why do we not invest the same emotions to peace narratives?

The following ICCT Research Paper "Responding to Cyber Jihad: Towards an Effective Counter Narrative" of March 2015 counter-narrative proposed: "Although religious leaders or religious associations might not consider it to be their core business, they could fulfill a role in explaining the values of Western society—the rule-of-law-based system, respect for human rights and the general policies adopted by governments—and the ways in which these values can be respected while still living the life of a devout Muslim."

Deconstructing the narrative, there are several red lights. The inherently pretentious and self-righteous attitude is part of the problem. In the age where whistle blowers thrive, where western societies reach their breaking points, where allies play the role of "Pharisee and tax collector" to their allies, the above narrative is simply penetrable. The king is naked and he has been stripped away of his royal clothing by his own people, not his enemy kings.

Could we imagine a peace-building story where "instead of these subject/heroes doing good things for others (the victims), the victims would do them for themselves. Would that not be the right form for a story about true bottom-up, locally-owned and empowering peace-building?"[12] In reality the presumably selfless heroes create passive recipients, and more often than not this dynamics are core to the master narratives of humanity. From bedtime stories with princes, dragons, and damsels in distress to the modern wars against the axis of evil.

Now we are reaching a point in history, where Eliade wonderfully described and insightfully foresaw,

an epoch, when humanity, to ensure its survival, finds itself reduced to desisting from any further "making" of history in the sense in which it began to make it from the creation of the first empires, confines itself to repeating prescribed archetypal gestures, and strives to forget, as meaningless and dangerous, any spontaneous gesture which might entail "historical" conse-

quences . . . For history either makes itself (as the result of the seed sown by
acts that occurred in the past, several centuries or even several millennia ago);
or it tends to be made by an increasingly smaller number of men who not only
prohibit the mass of their contemporaries from directly or indirectly interven-
ing in the history they are making (or which the small group is making), but in
addition have at their disposal means sufficient to force each individual to
endure, for his own part, the consequences of this history, that is, to live
immediately and continuously in dread of history. [13]

Modern man now is left with two options: (1) to oppose the history that is
being made by the very small minority (in this case he is free to choose
between suicide and deportation); (2) to take refuge in a subhuman existence
or in flight. [14] That is exactly what happens.

Master narratives of political discourse are setting up sequences of actions and events as routines and as such have a tendency to normalize, thereby giving guidance and directions to every day actions of subjects, without
which we would be lost. [15] Eliminating any freedom for action outside the
prescribed reality of the master narrative.

However, endorsing dominant and hegemonic narratives is often the same
as being complicit with the damage that these narratives bring. Although
"lives are lived and stories are told," [16] this analogy between story and life
has enabled insights on how narratives shape lives, almost creating self-
fulfilling prophesies. [17] In a way, the narratives bear the speaker's identity
and intentions; the creator of the narrative has the powerful opportunity to
pre-define people's lives. Those embracing the narratives are transformed to
storytellers themselves and then in turn they are transformed to the initial
creator's complicit. The only thing that could liberate us from being complicit is the lack of awareness and the lack of intent. But living in the age where
information society is a reality, negligence is criminal negligence no matter
what; for people cannot deny individual and collective responsibility anymore. Due diligence is an imperative for any citizen of the free world.

Nonetheless, from a psychoanalytical point of view, "self-esteem of a
people rises and falls with the fate of its nation. The nation and the idea of the
self are in many ways fused." [18] Complicity to master narratives could in
many ways be inevitable. It is part of human nature.

It has been often illustrated that nations, as a collective of individuals, have
difficulty accepting responsibility for aggression, and prefer to stress the pain
of their histories, the provocations which gave rise to warlike acts, their experience as victims, and the resulting justifications for their hostile behavior.
Rarely does a people acknowledge, for example, the aggression which must lie
behind the establishment of itself as a new nation or its expansion to fulfill the
collective myth of its territorial destiny. [19]

One has to accept and embrace the inherent traits of her own human nature and then accept with all fairness their existence in all humans, west and east of the map. Humans complying with legitimate governments or humans complying with terrorists or militia.

> Primitive meanings (not pathological) of motherhood and fatherhood are contained in the idea of the country or nation. Any political thinker who seeks a fellowship of all mankind beyond allegiances to nation states must recognize the psychological meaning of the identity of the self with the nation. Failure to do so will limit such concepts as the "brotherhood of man" to philosophical and Utopian visions and imaginings.[20]

One shall embrace human nature and its purgatory needs. One should embrace war and its narratives in order to truly understand, accept, and maybe even love humanity. That translating to acceptance that the same way we fear and reprimand the terrorists the same way the terrorist fears and reprimands us: the terrorists that took their land and killed their children (and as a matter of fact they/we did).

Not to disregard the psychoanalytical aspect of the war attractiveness to the human soul, Churchill's famous remark that "there is nothing so exhilarating as to be fired upon without result" captures the vigorous enthusiasm with which men may engage in war despite all the horrors which they bring about. "The only time members of my family have ever been happy, brave, successful, was in time of war," declares the contemporary southern grailseeker in Walker Percy's novel, Lancelot. Dr. Volkan pertains that war converts passivity and victimization into aggression and mastery. Worthless losers become glorious victors. Group purpose, a higher sense of one's collective and national cohesion, is achieved. The war leader becomes elevated as a symbolic national hero.[21]

One cannot build peace, cannot find harmony without before purging oneself in the feeling of deconstructing chaos. Humans are capable of breaking chaos into pieces and building cosmos. We are created "in the image and likeness of God" and we are either that or nothing at all.

Let There Be Peace

The willingness of the conflicting parties to accept the possibility of personal and communal suffering by initiation of violent conflict suggests, though, that if peace-building is to be successful, a deep understanding of the motivational dynamics driving them is needed.[22] As far as the Orient is concerned it has been suggested that due to historical reasons, there can be no stability, social progress, or constructive political developments without a deep understanding and enhancement of the role of religion. Eastern societies have a powerful and perplexed ontology, where secular and religious affairs intermingle. Hence, the regional and particular dynamics need to be considered in order to construct a peace-promoting counter-narrative.

The national, regional, and geopolitical dynamics in the Orient have been mostly negative.[23] These dynamics resulted in the creation of prejudices of the west towards them, associated with backwardness, poverty, and lack of freedom.[24] This perception of the region has had a twofold repercussion in the information of the locals' social identities: they have been self-justifying their violent behaviors as a part of their wild and adventurous past being revolutionaries against colonialism, or imperialism, or at least as a self-fulfilling prophecy; and they are retreating to conservatism and nationalism as a defensive mechanism, because the "others" are prejudiced against them.

These identity matrix has shaped one of the major defaults of the global society: delusional supra-national memories, which were informed by the winning parties' after every conflict. The problem is that in a global scale, in the realm of international politics and universal uber-narratives, there were no efforts for confrontation to pave the way towards transformation of society.[25] The patterns of consolidation have been presenting antagonistic political languages and different narratives of the recent past and previous conflicts. This fact, beyond any doubt, perpetuates confusion and rivalries.

In the uber-narrative of western prejudices that associate backwardness, poverty, and lack of freedom with the east. There is nowhere to be found an honest dialectic of how this alleged degradation arrived there. Are these people by nature incapable of democracy, peace and freedom? Was this condition created for them by the others residing in the land of democracy and freedom? If so, are they not responsible to fight their way to democracy and freedom? But what if they are viciously stopped by the others? In a world thrown into flames, a conspiracy theory is as good narrative as any and it is sought to be heard and seriously considered.

Current models for weak and fragile states identify these countries as deviations from a Weberian norm of institutionalized political authority. *They are defined by what they are not.* Such analysis fails to pay attention to what actually happens in such countries and how some of them successfully avoid or resolve conflict, despite not building strong institutions. It is preferable to analyze such countries in terms of the political processes that actually lead to certain outcomes.[26] Rather than deriving analysis and policy from universals drawn from moral impulses, one shall seek practical responses in the details of particular circumstances. Such an approach promises not only to be truer to reality, but also to provide the tools for more practically effective policies for prevention and reaction that should achieve better results.[27]

As illustrated in the preceding analysis, when peoples do find themselves in a state of self-defense intimidated by either severe economic recession or brutal conflicts and always tapped with lack of effective democratic political leadership, they react violently. They are retreating to their most conservative sodalities in order to find comfort and give meaning to what is happening to them and the society they belong. This applies for both sides of the conflict. As it is now, it applies to both west and east of the globe. How is religious fundamentalism different from political conservatism? How is Islamic extremism different from Christian fundamentalism? The motivation is the same: fear and survival instincts motivate.

In order to build an effective peace narrative examination of the intersection of social identity with individual identity is of great relevance, as even in social and generalized conflicts, there is a need to approach them in an individual basis because it is the only way to comprehend the motives and reverse them. As Marx pointed out, it is because of society (gesellschaft) that individuality exists, and vice versa. In fact, self-categorization theory suggests that individuals self-categorize with a certain social identity to the extent that the identity is prominent in the ongoing social context.[28] Adopting characteristics of the in-group prototype becomes normative: those characteristics prescribe what people ought to believe about own selves and how they should behave.

Collectivist cultures, or else high-context cultures, tend to define the group as "the basic unit of social perception; the self is defined in terms of in-group relationships; in-group goals have primacy or overlap with personal goals; in-group harmony is a value; and social behavior tends to be very different when the other person belongs to an in-group versus an out-group."[29]

The categorization of a society as collectivist is particularly important in the effort to understand the social dynamics of groups that have such an ideology, culture, and/or philosophy that aim to inform the identity of its members in a way that permeates all social contexts, not merely those in which the group's social identity is explicitly made salient. Religious groups are a good example of this. Although religion varies in salience from context to context, for true believers it cannot but pervade all aspects of their life. It provides for a set of norms, values, and beliefs whose validity and applicability are assumed and often claimed to be universal.[30]

Erikson[31] referred to religion as an important vector in the socio-historical matrix in which identity takes shape. He further argued that religion is the most long-standing institution that enhances fidelity, enduring commitment, and loyalty to an ideology that draws upon the meaningful and effective resolution of the psychosocial identity.[32] He explained that religion not only delineates a transcendent worldview emerging from moral behavioral norms in an idealistic base, but religious traditions also embody these norms and thus empower these norms, through the formation of a community of believers. Tzuriek also stated that religiosity has been demonstrated to predict commitment and purposefulness in identity.

The centrality of belief in belonging to religion was suggested by Emile Durkheim, who placed practice next to belief on a level of equal importance and argued that the most important part of religion was not the dogmas, nor even the deities, but the way in which those sharing common beliefs and rituals are acting together aiming to protect a greater entity such as community. Religious belief in that sense is whatever works best for individuals to give meaning and cohesion to an otherwise chaotic life.

Moreover, putting the divine in the center of the conflict has another benefit, which is to move the conflict from a psychology of scarcity to a psychology of surplus. Psychology of scarcity is based on an inner feeling that there is not enough to go around—if you do not grab you will be left with nothing and hungry.[33] The call to prayer—*Allah Akhbar*—highlights the spiritual dimension of the psychology of surplus. God is great; Allah has no limits. The same as the Greek God has, God shall take care. This spiritual attitude is one in which the divine is provided for all; no one will be left out or go hungry. What one gets is a gift at no one else's expense. Our response is not anxiety but thanksgiving. Thus we cannot emphasize enough the crucial importance of the psychology of surplus.

Thus, one needs to understand the identity dynamics in order to elaborate a constructive management model appropriate for each occasion. Social Identity Theory (SIT)[34] seeks to understand intergroup behavior by exploring how people use social categories to make sense of the world around them.[35] Hard conceptions of identity emphasize continuity across persons and time, whereas soft social constructionist perspectives argue identities are fragmented, multiple, and negotiable.[36] [37] Understanding how social identities are constructed gives conflict theorists a point of departure for theorizing how conflict resolution and transformation processes could be structured to influence meaning making; that produces open, interested, differentiated identities that are not oppositional in nature.[38]

The treatment of all the conflicting parties with empathy and understanding could be part only of a spiritual-based process. In order to truly resolve a conflict through a powerful narrative, it is essential to reconcile the different parties with each other and alleged perpetrators so all members can make amends with their past and function constructively within the society. This is also of great importance as far as the alleged wrongdoers of the conflict are concerned. The fear of being judged is very strong. One needs to take into account how natural human responses to harm and injustices may move people from being victims to becoming aggressors. These people suppress their grief as a way of hiding from shame, undermining their self-esteem, and sense of identity.[39] The egoism of victimization thus has two fundamental interrelated aspects: the justification of continuing hostility on the grounds of having been victimized by the other, and the narcissistic focusing of empathy upon one's own people with the consequent inability to identify with the suffering of the other group.[40]

Cloke[41] in his book *Mediating Dangerously* offers a quite interesting compilation of alternative definitions of a conflict, which could be of great relevance to narrative building. A conflict could represent "lack of awareness of the imminence of death; or inability to understand our essential interconnectedness within a community; or our own failures projected onto others; or a way to get attention and sympathy as the victim of evil; or the manifestation of contradictory forces coexisting in a single space; but primarily a demand for change in a system that has outlived its usefulness."

In a similar vein, Wedge said that social conflict that escalates into violence is the result of narcissistic rage, the pathology of the self whose destructive formations are inflicted upon the opposite group.[42] Cardinal aspect of the social conflicts and their supporting narratives, as indicated by the preceding definitions, appears to be the identity clash among oppositional groups.

All conflicts start with the reality that, while humankind is one species, people act as though we are divided into endless species. This is the phenomenon of pseudo-speciation defined by Erik Erikson (1969). Groups "provide their members with a firm sense of distinct and superior identity—and immortality."[43] In fact, a distinct feature of civil conflicts is that the rival groups develop a vested interest in maintaining the conflict as a raison d'être.[44]

Narratives supporting social violence disintegrate the foundations of the communal relationships[45] even at a global level. This disintegration occurs gradually as the dysfunctional organisms start personalizing systemic discord, through the promotion of identity polarization.[46] In the negotiation of identities lies the substance of the conflict and at the same time the means of its resolution; through the preservation of the societal cohesion by re-humanizing the other.

This largely applies in the construction of peace narratives. Only in the case where in need of a universal peace meta-narrative the narrator is the historian and the responsibility of fairness in the story to be created is greater than ever. And as historians confront a continuous reality from which they select a given set of events to be told, the events that are then employed by the historian through personal prioritization, organization, and linearization and turned into meaningful plots with recognizable characters with goals and motivations, a thread giving it overall unity, and a moral for the story.

And as G. Novack said, history is not the achievement of outstanding individuals, no matter how powerful, gifted or strategically placed but that of what "really constitutes the human race, the vast mass of families living for the most part on the fruits of their labor, which has been forgotten, and even of those who follow public professions, and work not for themselves but for society, who are engaged in teaching, ruling, protecting or healing others."[47]

The historian up to the task of making this new narrative has to transition himself to a prophet. As Nikos Kazantzakis in *The Last Temptation of Christ* said; "a prophet is the one who, when everyone else despairs, hopes. And when everyone else hopes, he despairs.[48] You'll ask me why. It's because he has mastered the Great Secret: that the Wheel turns." As human nature cannot alone explain the course of events or the characteristics of social life and as it is the changes in the conditions of life and labor that underlie the making and remaking of our human nature. A meta-historical narrative is in search.

SCENE III: THE END OF AN ERA

Common attitude in the narrative building appears to be that west has a humanitarian duty to export peace and stability, democracy and progress in the regions of the "wild" orient. The west it is not necessarily in a position to export any values or models of democracy. The west is not in the position to provide true freedom and democracy to their own constituency, let alone pretend to be masters of libertarianism to others. We tried it. We failed. Let us move on to alternative modes of conducting international politics. Let those people through their own processes inform the model of society and governance that fits their needs and particularities best. This concept could be precarious and ambivalent at best but there was a brief time in history where whole empires were not built on fear but acceptance of diversity.

De facto interdependency does not equal interventionism. There is no point in trying to prove whether these terrorist or anti-establishment ideologies are valid or not. History will show, assuming that there will be any objectivity to begin with. The key is to rather address the similar if not identical circumstances that not only allowed but demanded their creation.

As the oriental peoples have an inherent tendency—apparent through history—to incorporate the politicization of their inter-cultural contacts, their political mentality embraces the possibility of any cultural communication to be transformed into political act. Strong evidence for that is that western-type state of thick inter-institutional septum is not firmly established in the collective unconsciousness.

The aspect of religion was completely underestimated and marginalized in the process of westernization, as capitalistic models demand complete secularization. The capitalistic theory cannot possibly apply that simplistically as complete industrialization is yet to happen in the societies in question. Instead, economic recession is re-appearing with a disturbing frequency. People cannot rely upon sound and efficient states, which is partially the reason for the upsurge of religious extremism. The assumption that spirituality enables irrationality is exactly that: an assumption. It is not about the religious dogmas but about how people around the globe relate their religiosity and spirituality within the nation-state they belong.

Against the general approach of taking European developments as paradigmatic, atypical institutions and structures exist at particular points in time as the cumulative evolved result of agents' previous efforts to satisfy their needs and interests. Institutions are therefore more like artifacts than natural kinds.[49] They are the result of many individuals' purposive actions and unintended effects. To the extent there are common features of institutions these common features are derived from "parallel evolution"—a particular feature is a commonly accessible solution to a common existential problem—or the result of diffusion of organizational themes and ideas (transmission of governing styles and strategies).

It is also important to bear in mind that, at any given time, agents are presented with a repertoire of available institutions and variants (along the lines of Charles Tilly's point about a repertoire of strategies of collective action; Tilly 1986). The contents of the institutional repertoire are historically specific, reflecting the examples that are currently available and those that are available through historical memory.

THE END

Coming from the country that gave birth to democracy and now is deprived of democracy and indulged into anarchy, I can humbly say that a narrative is as good as the purpose is serves. When national constitutions are imposed by external actors and detached from the national and constitutional identity of the peoples, then democracy is as good as anarchy. In many cases people do not have a notion of statehood or nationhood and are not allowed to inform one. Rather, they are pawns in the global power game and anarchy is as good as democracy. A man I know once said to me in a conversation about Greek politics that when blood runs the streets like a river then, and only then, can we start talking about change of the rotten status quo, as then and only then, people's mentality is forced to change. Then, and only then, an era ends. What I understand from that quote is that peace shall not arrive unless we repent our collective failures. So far humans have not done this without violent outbreaks. If that is true, let it then be: change is needed. A different meta-narrative is needed. We have to confront our demons and with an open heart and fairness approach the other. For this world we live is a kingdom of consciousness or nothing at all.

NOTES

1. From Minucius Felix, Octavius, R. E. Wallis, trans. in The Ante-Nicene Fathers (Buffalo, N. Y.: The Christian Literature Publishing Co., 1887), Vol. 4, pp. 177-178.

2. Cassie Brandes, "The Social Psychology of Radical Martyrdom Culture," Martyrdom Project (University of Oregon, 2013).

3. T. Vinson and D. Mcdonnell D., "War Narratives, Applied Theatre Researcher," *IDEA Journal*, Issue 8, 2007.

4. Ibid.

5. Cassie Brandes, "The Social Psychology of Radical Martyrdom Culture," Martyrdom Project (University of Oregon, 2013).

6. Ibid.

7. Dominik Güss, Teresa Tuason, and Vanessa Teixeira, "A Cultural-psychological Theory of Contemporary Islamic Martyrdom," *Journal for the Theory of Social Behaviour* 37 (2007): 415-445.

8. Neil Whitehead and Nasser Abufarha, "Suicide, Violence, and Cultural Conceptions of Martyrdom in Palestine." *Social Research* (2008) 75, 395-416.

9. Z Barakat (2009), "Diverging Narratives as Part of the Conflict; Converging Narratives as Part of the Solution," (presentation, Religious Narratives on Jerusalem and Their Role in Peace Building Proceedings of an Interreligious Conference, Jerusalem, Israel, October 20, 2015).

10. Mircea Eliade, translation of *Le Mythe de Veternel Retour: Archetypes et Repetition* (Paris: Librairie Gallimard, 1949).

11. Ibid.

12. Eneko Sanz, Ed. Jeremy Tomlinson, "The Peace Building Story" (paper, CPCS Peace Practitioners' Research Conference, 2012).

13. Mircea Eliade, translation of *Le Mythe de Veternel Retour: Archetypes et Repetition* (Paris: Librairie Gallimard, 1949).

14. Ibid.

15. Michael Bamberg, *Considering Counter Narratives: Narrating, Resisting, Making Sense.* (Amsterdam: John Benjamins Publishing Company, 2004), 351-371). Amsterdam: John Benjamins.,

16. Ibid.

17. Paul Ricoeur, *Oneself as Another,* (Chicago: University of Chicago Press, 1990).

18. J Mack forward to Vamik Volkan, *Cyprus-War and Adaptation: A Psychoanalytic History of Two Ethnic Groups in Conflict* (University Press of Virginia, 1979).

19. Ibid.

20. Ibid.

21. Ibid.

22. Marieke Kleiboer, "Understanding Success and Failure of International Mediation," *The Journal of Conflict Resolution* 40 no 2 (2013), 360-389.

23. Lisen Bashkurti, "Political Dynamics within the Balkans: The Cases of Bosnia and Herzegovina, Macedonia, Bulgaria, Serbia, and Montenegro," (Chicago: Chicago-Kent College of Law, 2004), 49.

24. Michael Radu, "Why Eastern and Central Europe Look West," *Orbis* 41:1 (1997), 39.

25. John Paul Lederach, *Building Peace: Sustainable Reconciliation in Divided Societies,* (Washington, D.C.: United States Institute of Peace Press, 1997).

26. Alex de Waal, Jens Meierhenrich, and Bridget Conley-Zilkich, "How Mass Atrocities End: An Evidence-Based Counter-Narrative," *The Fletcher Forum of World Affairs* (2012).

27. Ibid.

28. Henri Tajfel and John Turner, "An Integrative Theory of Intergroup Conflict," *Relations: Essential Readings: Key Readings in Social Psychology,* (New York: Psychology Press, 2011), 94-109.

29. Peter Carnevale and Dong-Won Choi, "Culture in the Mediation of International Disputes," *International Journal Of Psychology* 35: 2, (2000) 105-110.

30. Tom Postmes and Anton Jetten, *Individuality and the Group Advances in Social Identity*, (London: SAGE Publications, 2006).

31. Erik Erikson, *Gandhi's Truth: On the Origin of Militant Non-Violence*, (New York: Norton, 1969), 431.

32. Ibid.

33. Dr. Amirav M. & Dr. Abramovitch H. (2009), Recovering the Holiness of Jerusalem: A New Approach to an Old Conflict, in Religious Narratives on Jerusalem and Their Role in Peace Building Proceedings of an interreligious conference held October 20th, in Jerusalem

34. Henri Tajfel and John Turner, "An Integrative Theory of Intergroup Conflict," *Relations: Essential Readings: Key Readings in Social Psychology*, (New York: Psychology Press, 2011), 94-109.

35. P Oakes, "Psychological Groups and Political Psychology: A Response to Huddy's "'Critical Examination of Social Identity Theory.'" *Political Psychology*, 2002.

36. Rogers Brubaker, *Citizenship and Nationhood in France and Germany*, (Cambridge: Harvard University Press, 1992).

37. Stephen Goodwin, " From UN Safe Havens to Sacred Spaces: Contributions of Religious Sodalities to Peace Building and Reconciliation in Post-War Bosnia and Herzegovina," *Studies in World Christianity* 9:2, 171-188.

38. Dennis D.J. Sandole, Sean Byrne, Ingrid Sandole-Staroste, and Jessica Senehi, *Handbook of Conflict Analysis and Resolution*, (London: Routledge, 2009).

39. Martha Minow, *Between Vengeance and Forgiveness*, (New York: Doubleday Press, 1999).

40. J Mack forward to Vamik Volkan, *Cyprus-War and Adaptation: A Psychoanalytic History of Two Ethnic Groups in Conflict* (University Press of Virginia, 1979).

41. Kenneth Cloke, *Mediating Dangerously: the Frontiers of Conflict Resolution*, (San Francisco: Jossey-Bass, 2001).

42. Kevin Avruch, *Culture and Conflict Resolution: Contributions in Ethnic Studies*, (Washington, D.C.: USIP Book Press, 1998).

43. J.V. Montville, (2002). "Religion and Peace Making." In R. G. Helmick & R. L. Peterson (Eds.), *Forgiveness and Reconciliation: Religion, Public Policy and Conflict Transformation* (Philadelphia: Templeton Foundation Press, 2002).

44. Ibid.

45. Mishra Kumar, *Beyond the Cold War*, Chapter 1: "Civil War Civil Peace," (London: Pluto Press, 1998).

46. Kenneth Cloke, *Mediating Dangerously: the Frontiers of Conflict Resolution*, (San Francisco: Jossey-Bass, 2001).

47. George Novack, *Understanding History Major Theories Of History, From The Greeks To Marxism*, (Australia: Resistance Books, 2002).

48. Nikos Kazatzakis, *The Last Temptation of Christ*, (London: Bruno Cassirer, 1960).

49. Daniel Little, "Explaining Large-Scale Historical Change," Understanding Society blog.

Chapter Four

National Strategy on a Dollar

Finding a Civil-Military Principle
for Coordinating Peace and Security

Christopher Holshek

One thing the low-intensity conflict world between peace and war the United States and other major powers have long inhabited has shown is that it is not either/or but both. While soft power has rightly gained currency and relevance since 9/11, and it is clear that military and other forms of coercive power are not the most efficacious, inexpensive, and low-risk means of expressing national interest, the opposite conclusion could be equally dangerous. Persuasive and coercive forms of national power are not substitutes for each other—they are not mutually exclusive and, in fact, are often most impactful and sustainable when combined. While the implications are both strategic and operative, the real challenge is not whether to apply hard or soft power, but how to balance, align, and apply them—coordination.

Indeed, there are many lessons that can be drawn from what the Pentagon has called the Decade of War[1] and David Rothkopf of *Foreign Policy* has dubbed the Decade of Fear[2] that leads to a greater emphasis on soft power. Overwhelming force applied unilaterally and without appropriate diplomatic context has proved disastrous at best, implying a need for more comprehensive, collaborative, connective, and coordinated approaches to issues of peace and security. An equally important insight is that the peace-wars since 9/11 have elucidated "a pathological American problem—the United States knows well how to get into wars, and fight them, but not how to end them."[3]

Another insight is the longstanding penchant for throwing money at the problem, the irresistible focus on operations and tactics in stability operations, counterinsurgency, counterterrorism, or winning hearts and minds, and the conflation of military deterrence with conflict prevention. These operational concepts have all been substitutes for strategy rather than strategies themselves. This tactical mindset "dominates national security decision-making prioritizes military means over political ends and confuses activity with progress," former member of the Defense Policy Board Nadia Schadlow noted.[4] For that reason, "the United States vacates the space between war and peace." This also explains why discussion of US responses to violent extremist organizations like the Islamic State is almost predominantly kinetic. The military response to the (non-military) Ebola crisis in West Africa or how security assistance efforts have been almost exclusively on training up partner forces in near mirror-image of US military culture. Compounding the perception of US heavy-handedness is the increased dependency on unmanned aerial vehicles for surveillance and targeting of outlier threats to US national security. For many, this is the face of American engagement abroad.

Americans in general have been averse to thinking and acting strategically because previously they could get away with it—as said in sports, they have been more "lucky than good." This comes in part from the American political culture of short-term focus on election and budgetary cycles as well as the tendency to view foreign engagement largely through the prism of the Pentagon. American power applied abroad is almost exclusively a function of military power whose organizational culture sees its use in terms of total rather than limited war in what Russell Weigley's seminal work, *The American Way of War*, called a strategy of annihilation. The strategy is characterized by zero-sum terms such as "victory" that often drive military escalation well beyond political imperatives, as was seen in Vietnam.[5]

Ignorance-based politics and a consumerist approach to increasingly complex and enduring issues of peace and security are bad for business, in many ways, for a great power still struggling to shape world events rather than be shaped by them. America's trademark splendid isolationism has gone from a quant nuisance to a strategic liability, seriously draining its national power and international standing and leaving public constituencies wide-open to manipulation by everyone from politicians, the media, and violent extremist organizations. These actors exploit flash-bang sensationalism that affect a tiny number Americans, such as terrorism and infectious diseases to irresponsibly fever angst—a siege mentality—and self-styled superiority. Moreover, the fact that "they know more about us than we know about them"— politically, culturally, and economically as well as militarily—is now a major grand strategic vulnerability.[6]

All of this is indicative of the much larger challenge of seeing the forest for the trees, or what has been called a strategy deficit reflected in an outdated national security paradigm. This is predicated on seeing national security as the über alles [7] of American intervention, intelligence programs, and an imbalanced Cold War era interpretation of the fundamental civil-military relationship in American society that persists today. Both strategically and closer to the ground, the civil-military nexus of peace and security is more relevant than ever. The US civil-military approach to foreign policy and national security needs an overhaul not just because of the costly, counter-productive, and unsustainable overreliance on hard power and the underutilization of soft power but because its persistent misalignment and malformation threatens to accelerate American decline, at home as well as abroad.

In policy and practice and at both levels of application, national strategy applied through civil-military coordination[8] has to walk the talk of American values. National values largely shape national interests, whereas national interests, in turn inform policy, operations, and tactics. Such is the hierarchy of national strategy, characterized by its political narrative. "Narrative," Dr. Ajit Maan explains, "is a rendering of events, actions, and characters in a certain way for a certain purpose. The purpose is persuasion. The method is identification."[9] Narrative is really a reflection of who one is and what one is about—identity and values in the field of action—on personal and collective levels. National narratives work for a time, but when the paradigm shifts, they do not work as well anymore, requiring update. The paradigm has obviously shifted.

A TALE OF TWO CENTURIES

The global context for civil-military coordination at all levels has changed. The national security paradigm, which identifies security as primarily that of the state, has become a less effective organizing construct for security. Top-down, power-driven Western notions of national sovereignty and security of the 20th century are less relevant than the emerging, values-based, bottom-up human security actualities that have been gaining ascendency since the fall of the Berlin Wall. In other words, the referent for security in a world in which power is more distributed is increasingly the individual or community rather than the state.[10]

World War I was the last major war in which the majority of casualties were military. From World War II on, as many as four-fifths of casualties have been civilians. As irregular warfare gained precedence, the center of gravity of modern armed conflict has likewise decentralized. In a flatter, more interconnected world, the power is in the people. To its credit, what the military has come to realize faster and more thoroughly than any other part of the US government is that the solutions to the peace-wars of today are not primarily found in their profession.

The low success rate of US and Western military-led conflict transformation and security assistance efforts since especially the turn of the century is attributable to two things: a failure to comprehend the security sector as a function of governance and civil society and an ill appreciation of the civil-military relationship as the critical locus of peace and security.

It starts by understanding that the drivers of conflict and instability rather than threats are the more elemental and systemic causality of conflict: the disease in relation to the symptoms. Illicit power structures and cultures of impunity demonstrate the most persistent and nettlesome drivers of conflict and challenges to conflict transformation and transition from fragile states and weak civil societies. These drivers are largely astride the security sector and the civil-military relationship. Poor governance and weak civil society institutions, a feeble sense of national identity, and socioeconomic shortfalls especially with respect to youth and women have created the conditions that illicit activities such as transnational drug and human trafficking and especially terrorist networks have exploited. "ISIS got so big because of the failure of governance in Syria and Iraq to deliver the most basic services," Francis Fukiyama pointed out: "ISIS is not strong. Everything around it was just so weak."[11]

Most drivers of conflict are, in fact, civil society problems. As in many countries, according to the Center for Media Peace Initiatives, "the eminent explosion caused by the lack of a future for Nigeria's youth will be more deadly than Boko Haram."[12] If regional stability is the overarching interest of the United States in the Middle East, then the region's "massive demographic shift" is driving destabilization more than the terrorist networks that exploit these conditions.[13] The UN estimates over half the population of Syria needs humanitarian assistance, while Syrian refugees comprise over one-quarter of the populations of Lebanon and Jordan.[14] The response of the US, the west, and the Arab world so far has not been "commensurate with the enormity of the suffering," as Fareed Zakaria put it mildly.[15]

Shortfalls, in turn, in what the US Institute of Peace has called "security sector governance" and civil society are no doubt chief among causal factors that led to the 2012 coup in Mali, the rapid roll-through of the Islamic State in Iraq and Syria, and the success of separatist forces serving as proxies to Russia non-linear destabilization efforts in Ukraine. In all these cases, government-sponsored defense, police, and other security forces were unable to prevent the takeover of over broad swaths of real estate inside of internationally recognized borders. In Mali, the surprisingly swift collapse of what was perceived to be one of Africa's more enduring democracies was due more to internal than external factors. In Nigeria, the greater de-stabilizing force has not been Boko Haram, whose issues are largely community-based, but the Nigerian security forces. Indeed, the security forces of such vulnerable states have been poorly led, equipped, organized, and trained as well as fragmented and incapable of keeping their soldiers from committing atrocities or untoward acts against their own civilians. In numerous instances, reports have also indicated that some military officers and other officials may be linked to the drug trade and other illicit activities. The security sector can therefore be as much a source of the core problem in weak and fragile states as the solution. Time and again, poor civil-military relations evidenced by the behavior of one's own security forces pose an even greater challenge than threats like externally supported violent extremists organizations.

If going after the drivers of conflict and instability rather than the threats emanating from them is really the game at hand, that requires a capability found less in the military and more resident in civilian agencies like the State Department and the likewise chronically under-resourced US Agency for International Development and its NGO partners, as well as international organizations like the United Nations or regional organizations such as the African Union. In contemporary conflict management, military power is supporting and not supported. The way to defeat illicit powers and violent extremist organizations is not to wage war against their operators as much as to wage peace against the sources of their power.

The constraints of this transformation of the strategic and operational environments, converging with the restraints of growing resource shortages, have correspondingly shifted the functioning paradigm for humanitarian relief and development organizations as much as for the military, with associated changes in the approach to the civil-military nexus as a whole.

From a broader perspective, the fundamental shift in the international order between the 20th and 21st centuries has been more inflective than intrinsic, particularly in the balance and interplay between what has been called soft and hard power. National power in both its source and application is characterized by an industrial-era, state-centric, top-down, zero-sum, empirical, and calculable game of war and peace played largely by diplomats and soldiers, interest-driven, and manifested mostly in hard currency and armies. It reached its zenith in the late 20th century. What is now beginning to hold greater sway is influence derived from national, societal, and organizational strengths, rather than state-centric power: post-industrial, bottom-up, and values-based involving myriad non-state and intra-state actors across an ambiguous spectrum (or cycle) of conflict and peace and associated complexities. In this new "ecosystem," Napoleon's apparent observation that "in war, the moral is to the physical as three is to one" takes on an even more appropriate meaning.

Concentrated military, financial and other forms of coercive power are the vestiges of a Westphalian state-centric international order. But what now increasingly characterizes that order is the struggle for power and identity among state and non-state organizations and networks in the spaces between war and peace and beyond and between states, amplified and accelerated by the 24/7 media and social networks that make the narrative predominant. In the 21st century, coercive power is losing both its dominance and appropriateness. Hard power is more threats-based, resource-intensive, zero-sum, reactive, and short-term (i.e. tactical). It is, however, faster acting, more controllable, and more measurable. Soft power, in turn, is more suitable to collaborative, human security settings. It is community-based, largely resident in civil society and the private sector, and is more adaptable, economical, renewable, engaging, synergistic, and durable (i.e. strategic). It is normally slower to take effect across a broad, unpredictable front, although social networking technologies as of late have had accelerating and amplifying effects.

This is not to say that hard power is obsolete—just no longer as overriding. In truth, this re-balancing is a return to a historical American grand strategic equilibrium predating the Cold War. Despite NSC-68's emphasis on diplomacy's continued lead in American grand strategy and George F. Kennan's refrain to "first use moral authority," the militarization of applied American power in the latter half of the 20th century had soft power (in policies, programs, budgets, and operations) functioning more as a force multiplier. In form as well as function, the face of US foreign policy has been largely a military one. In truth, what brought down the Berlin Wall was the tipping point of rising expectations of Eastern Europeans (not unlike the social unrest seen in many places today) while allied military power contained the Soviets. In other words, hard power was the holding—or containing—action while soft power was the offensive dynamic. NATO's vast arsenals enabled what NSC-68 called the "corrosive power of freedom" to go to work on the self-contradictions of the Soviet state over time. Self-determination, a principle internationalized by Woodrow Wilson during World War I, was the moral impetus. With the collapse of that order, the re-contextualization, re-alignment, and re-balancing of applied power that should have happened as far back as 1989 is now a blinding flash of the obvious.

This epochal reality is truer for the United States than any other country, as the world's only global power for the last generation. But its national strategic style goes much further back in history. Since the Civil War, the US has looked to win its wars, deter its adversaries, and assure its allies through overwhelming industrial and technological superiority predicated on an astounding abundance of land, labor, energy, and cheap capital. It could afford a wasteful, surplus mentality. Since 1945, it had been the dominant power in the world. It could afford its own, 19th-century interpretation of sovereignty and exceptionalism while everyone else was internationalizing. In other words, America had succeeded in globalizing everything but itself.

For the first time in its history the US is entering a newfound era of relative strategic scarcity. It can no longer take an abundance of resources for granted. The economic and financial basis of traditional state-centric power is diminishing through a globalization process that the US itself has largely set in motion. Beyond reducing America's throw-weight in general, it is translating into an end of unilateral freedom of action. Asymmetric threats and the rise of regional powers have already been mitigating longstanding US advantages, while global competitors can now better bankroll their own agendas. Perhaps most importantly, information and social networking technologies and low-cost, socio-cultural enterprises now present inexpensive equalizers to older, more costly, and more centralized industrial-era forms of power. The moral, or psychological, is now plainly ascendant over the physical.

The upshot to all this is that it may force Americans to think and act more strategically. Strategy, after all, is fundamentally about making choices about the future, and a strategic mindset is driven mostly by scarcity. (If you can do everything, and you dominate the scene, you don't have to make choices; so, you can just react rather than look ahead.) In the 21st century, there will be no dominant power. Although the United States will remain the leading power for decades to come, its ability to wield especially more traditional state-centric forms of power will be much more constrained and restrained by factors less and less under its span of control. Indeed, the heyday of state-centric power in the new international arena is diminishing. Power is dissipating into more distributed forms. As the upheavals in the Middle East and North Africa are demonstrating, the dynamic is now more about the strength, influence, and reach of ideas, globally archetypical but community-based. More importantly, it is about how these ideas communicate to work in people's lives. In one word: innovation. In fact, the power of nation-states alone is becoming less relevant than the influence of people and organizations networked outside of and within governments. The sources of this are largely in civil society.

Along with the changed context for national and international power is the changed nature of security. Even more in Africa than Afghanistan, the most important element of Clausewitz's remarkable trinity— the people, not the government or the army— is the ultimate arbitrator in war and peace. Making good on that potential requires more than understanding that "the future of war is about winning people, not territory," or "leaving behind an outmoded view of nation-on-nation warfare."[16] It requires empowering people more than politicians, and pursuing peace and justice with the same energy as engaging enemies.

This emerging civil-military enterprise, called "human security" 20 years ago in the United Nations Development Program's *Human Development Report*, introduced a dialectic to the conventional national security paradigm.

> Human security is about the security of the tribe, the community, and, above all, the individual. It is a democratization of the concept of security. Human security has emerged as the alter ego of national security mainly because, as President Obama has pointed out, "technology and globalization has put power once reserved for states in the hands of individuals." Unlike national security's

fixation with threats, human security's concern is with the drivers of conflict—the difference between treating symptoms and curing the disease, or preventing its outbreak in the first place. One is primarily tactical; the other is more strategic.[17]

It is the lack of empowerment at the retail more than the wholesale level that spawns violent extremist networks in the Middle East or Africa or enables Russia to run roughshod in Ukraine. Waves of popular unrest in response to everything from jobs, food prices, public pensions, poor educational and job opportunities, wealth disparities, mass migrations re-drawing maps. They also re-define national societies and energy and the climate change evince a groundswell of discontent with political elites to deliver on socioeconomic fundamentals and essential public services.

> The underlying causes in failed leadership and authoritarianism, inadequate governance and corruption, demographics and a massive youth bulge and unemployment problem in the various Arab Development Reports have all gotten worse since the upheavals that began in 2011. The religious and ideological struggles that interact with these underlying causes now spread from the Philippines to Morocco, and from Sub-Saharan Africa to the Islamic portions of Russia and China, explained Center for Strategic and International Studies Burke Chair of Strategy Anthony Cordesman.[18]

Moreover, governance is more than government. Government refers to formal state structures, largely top-down, whereas governance refers to both formal and informal power structures comprising civil society and residing mostly in tribes and communities, largely bottom-up. The security sector is a matter of governance and civil society, sustainable as well as successful security sector assistance contributes best to good governance of the security sector by clearly communicating to security forces in partner nations the benefits of a healthy civil-military relationship, civil authority over security forces whose general management is largely transparent and as legislative as executive, and the role of security forces in protecting the people and not just the state. It operationalizes democracy.

Security, prosperity, and social welfare are increasingly intertwined, making it everybody's business. In the American psyche, security was something that happened "over there." But in an intricate global ecosystem where events have worldwide ripple effects in a matter of hours, this is all changing. The image of America, in turn, is being more widely and rapidly transmitted to other societies. Over here matters over there, as much as over there matters over here.

Comprehensive and collaborative approaches to conflict prevention and post-conflict operations in multilateral, human security settings are everyday for civil society organizations working there and elsewhere. They stress the long-term, legitimacy, and relationship-building characteristics of development. In this more normative paradigm, development, appropriately done, is therefore not a component of security: it is the basis of it. This is vital to understanding the difference from security in the 21st century not as simply an expansion of the state-centric national security paradigm into social disciplines—which seems to be the current interpretation in the US government, which sees development policy more as an instrument of foreign policy and national security interests, aimed at the proliferation of *pax americana*.

The growing limitations of hard power commensurate with the rise of the efficacies of soft power, increasing inter-connectivity of global communities, the integration of security and development, and burgeoning resource restraints are driving more comprehensive, collaborative, and coordinated approaches. The re-contextualization, re-balancing, and proper alignment of the civil-military nexus remain at the locus of international intervention, whether for humanitarian, development, or reasons of state interest.

American strategy, policy, and operations have been flawed of late because they still run on 20th century operating software that leaves it dangerously out of touch with the times. The only serious upgrades to the National Security Act of 1947 have been the Foreign Service Act of 1961 and the Goldwater-Nichols Act of 1986. This strategic software suite no longer adequately processes two emergent systemic imperatives. First are the constraints of a complex and hyper-connected 21st century environment in which the power of persuasion is increasingly more relevant than that of coercion and where the security of individuals and communities underwrites the security of states – and where both are as distributed as they are centralized. Then there are the restraints of diminishing strategic resources, especially financial, in the face of these broader and more complex challenges to a wider understanding of security.

The issue is really not as much strategic ambitions as a strategic style still predicated on Weigley's "strategy of annihilation" and industrial-era strategic thinking. As those writing about network-centric warfare have already critiqued:

Accordingly, our American fixation has been the technical and industrial means of waging war. Our collective over-awe at the significance of our industrial achievements often leads us to expect strategic effects from systems and capabilities for tactical or operational impact. The result is a growing imbalance between our current capabilities and the range of security challenges for which our technology isn't the sole answer.[19]

In fiscal terms, US taxpayers have been getting increasingly less bang for the buck. According to a Harvard University study, the wars in Iraq and Afghanistan have cost the nation somewhere between $4-6 trillion in total direct and associated costs, without commensurate strategic gain. Programs like the F-35 Joint Strike Fighter that run in the trillions are producing ineffective platforms, requiring recall of much older aircraft like the A-10 proving more adept at going after the likes of the Islamic State, evincing a badly broken military procurement system.

The American national security paradigm, predicated on an interpretation of the fundamental civil-military relationship in American society forged under the exigencies of the Cold War era and revitalized since 9/11 explains why most US civil-military approaches to applied foreign and national security policy are correspondingly out of synch. Beyond Eisenhower's prescient warning about the military-industrial complex, Americans have grown accustomed to a vast national security state that, with the war on terrorism, permeates life at home and not just in policies abroad. Rothkopf's Decade of Fear derives from a culture driven by a relentless search for enemies that seems embedded in the national DNA.

> I don't mean a search in the sense of ferreting them out and defeating them. I mean that America seems to have a visceral need for them. Many in the United States have a rampant, untreated case of enemy dependency. Politicians love enemies because bashing them helps stir up public sentiment and distract attention from problems at home. The defense industry loves enemies because enemies help them make money. Pundits and their publications love enemies because enemies sell papers and lead eyeballs to cable-news food fights.[20]

The grand strategic vulnerability of American insularity stems largely from a domestic version of this enemy addiction in hyper-partisanship at home. As a result, "foreign policy and national security have become useful partisan cudgels precisely because the public has limited understanding of them and thus gravitates to caricatures."[21] The obsession with instant gratification, in turn, "has pressed US strategy toward an ever-greater reliance on the military element of national power."[22] Pile on the "mental illness problem, along with a poverty problem, a violence problem, a racism problem, and a policing problem," all indicative of low levels of collaboration, and the U.S begins to look more like the kind of failing state it looks to send its troops to.[23] The poorer state of civil-military relations should thus be no wonder.

THE FAULT LIES NOT IN OUR STARS . . .

Most scholars and commentators on the subject of the civil-military relationship in the United States turn first to Samuel Huntington's seminal work, *The Soldier and the State*, to begin discussion. It is more fitting to go back nearly two more centuries prior, to the Constitution of the United States, whose division of powers and authority, along with its system of check and balances, "has succeeded not only in defending the nation against all enemies foreign and domestic, but in upholding the liberty it was meant to pre-serve."[24] The American way of the civil-military relationship is thus funda-mental not only to the profession of arms; rather, it is fundamental to American civil society:

> Civil-military relations in a democracy are a special application of representa-tive democracy with the unique concern that designated political agents con-trol designated military agents. Acceptance of civilian supremacy and control by an obedient military has been the core principle of the American tradition of civil-military relations. Their client is American [civil] society, which has entrusted the officer corps with the mission of preserving the nation's values and national purpose. Ultimately, every act of the American military profes-sional is connected to these realities he or she is in service to the citizens of a democratic state who bestow their trust and treasure with the primary expecta-tion that their state and its democratic nature will be preserved.[25]

This was by and large the civil-military consensus in the United States until after World War II. Until then, the typical pattern was to maintain a small, professional force that could be augmented in the event of national emergency through the militia (today's Reserve and National Guard), thus tempering the general distrust of the military (reflected, arguably, in the Second Amendment). In the wake of World War II, for the first time in US history, a large, standing (and eventually professional) peacetime military force has existed. Huntington's book appeared in 1957, the same year as *Sputnik*, when also for the first time in its history, the US was faced with the clear and present danger of nuclear Armageddon.

Given this historic departure and the existential exigencies of the Cold War, Huntington's interpretation of the civil-military relationship is under-standable. Paradoxically (or perhaps ironically), Huntington concluded that to preserve democracy, society should grant the military substantial autono-my in managing international violence, in exchange for submission to civil-ian direction. For his theories, critics excoriated Huntington as overly mili-tant, students staged protests during lectures, and Harvard fired him.[26] Hunt-ington's model, which suspended the traditional consensus and balance of the American civil-military relationship, made more sense under the condi-tions of the Cold War and the international order it maintained. Once those conditions changed and that order began to break down, however, first with the fall of the Berlin Wall and then resuming with the difficulties of applied American power in the post-9/11 years (as explained above), the inherent flaws of Huntington's model became increasingly obvious: "the most signifi-cant shortcoming of Huntington's construct was its failure to recognize that a separation between political and military affairs is not possible—particularly at the highest levels of policymaking."[27] In other words:

Huntington's claim that an autonomous military profession should [sic.] develop its expertise free from outside involvement is also problematic. For one
thing, it underestimates the impact of service culture and service parochialism.
Left to their own devices, the services may focus on the capabilities they
would like to have rather than the capabilities the country needs. Even beyond
this concern, an emphasis on autonomy heightens the risk of creating a military unable to meet the requirements set out in the US military's own doctrine,
which talks of the need to integrate all instruments of national power [six.] to
further US national interests . . . Effective partnerships in war are likely to
require collaborative education, training, planning and capabilities . . . This
logic led Huntington to the extraordinary argument in his concluding chapter
that the solution was for American society to become less liberal and more like
the military in its culture and values. This proposed solution is extraordinary
because it is a clear reversal of ends–means logic: instead of the military
serving to protect American values, American society should change its values
to serve the interest of military effectiveness. [28]

This idea of the military as social role model is not so arcane. President
Obama expressed similar ideas in his 2012 State of the Union address. After
lauding the achievements of the armed forces, he said: "At a time when too
many of our institutions have let us down, they exceed all expectations.
They're not consumed with personal ambition. They don't obsess over their
differences. They focus on the mission at hand. They work together. Imagine
what we could accomplish if we followed their example." [29] With the popularity of the military in American society at an all-time high and that of
politicians at an all-time low, the civil-military societal imbalance that began
with the Second World War is now over seven decades old:

The psychology of civil–military apartheid and anonymous adoration of the
military is intrinsically undemocratic and elitist. Our decision in 1972 to pay
the economic rather than social costs of the historic anomaly of a large standing peacetime army has resulted in an increasingly professional but correspondingly disconnected warrior class. And the more disconnected they are
from us, the more we have been willing to use them in an era of perpetual
warfare against terrorism or for reasons such as humanitarian intervention. [30]

A national decision that once took a declaration of war or an act of
Congress is now an executive order authorizing a drone strike. It absolves us,
as the Brookings Institute's Phil Klay laid out, of the moral dilemmas and
public debates essential to defining the political parameters on the use of
force on our behalf. [31] But this "a matter of failed citizenship as it is failed
politics." [32]

This decoupling and distortion of the traditional American democratic
civil-military relationship is not only manifest in domestic social politics or
the horizontal dysfunctions of interagency and civil-military coordination, it
has also contributed to a vertical imbalance with an overemphasis on opera-

tions and tactics, leading to what the strategist Colin S., Gray has called "a persistent strategy deficit" in the US, pointing out that: "If you do not really function strategically, it does not much matter how competent you are at regular, or irregular, warfare—you are not going to collect the political rewards that American blood and money have paid for." [33] Interestingly, Gray points out that the "awesome" tactical power and performance of the US military, in contrast to its strategic retardation, is similar to that of Germany's *Wehrmacht* during World War II. The vertical disparity between policy and operations is thus very real, underscoring the connection between the global and the local, between the strategic and the tactical:

> As military organizations expand their work into civil governance areas, it is not only the distinction between soldiers and civilians that blurs. It is also the social coding that military and nonmilitary agents use to describe the military organization and its particular ethos and rationality. As a result, it become unclear what kind of organization the military is and what it could and should be used for. It becomes difficult to communicate in an exact manner about military affairs. [34]

In truth, the alignment of civil and military inflections of power and influence has always been the central challenge to anyone and everyone involved in trying to prevent, mitigate, or manage conflict and enforce, keep, or build peace. In the 21st century, however, this locus has only grown in significance. Context being what it is, if there is to be a paradigm shift in civil-military approaches—viewed from both sides—more in line with the emerging *Zeitgeist*, then two fundamental realities must be appreciated. First, civil-military coordination, at any level, is inherently thinking globally. Second, to be both effective and credible, civil-military coordination must be an application of the democratic civil-military relationship that is morally consistent and symmetric with the national narrative.

With respect to the first insight, when looking from the more global, human security vantage point of the 21st century, a more comprehensive and collaborative understanding of civil-military engagement becomes possible. As such, context takes precedence over content, partnership more than predominance, strategy more than operations and tactics, and human more than organizational enterprises.

This has no doubt especially true in the culturally charged Muslim world, where the United States, having broken the eggs of autocracy in Iraq, can perhaps help Arab civil society make the omelet of self-governance, albeit in a more indirect, limited, and longer-term way. In this sense, therefore, the most important lesson of the war in Iraq is not that better planning, operational approaches, and tactics may have changed its outcome. "Instead, the real solution is re-thinking American grand strategy." [35]

"MILITARY CIVICS" AND ADAPTIVE LEADERSHIP

Unless viewed strategically, as a development challenge more than simply addressing national security threats, civil-military coordination will never be seen and seized as an opportunity rather than a problem. The primacy of civil authority, among other democratic principles, is at the crux of peace and security, democratization, and capacity development in security assistance in conflict areas. Both strategic and operational in application as well as outcome, it best gets to the real drivers of conflict and thus reduces the vulnerabilities emblematic of weak and fragile states that violent extremist organizations look to exploit in the first place.

Establishing a strong, sustainable civil-military relationship in host nations that institutionalizes the primacy of civil authority and takes a more strategic, peacebuilding approach to security sector development is the key component of conflict transformation as well as security assistance. It must be integral to all international security assistance efforts. If the center of gravity of long-term peace and stability is effective governance and human as well as state-level security, and the central nexus of a broader security sector is the civil-military relationship, then establishing a strong, sustainable civil-military relationship that institutionalizes the primacy of civil authority and links security sector development to civil society peacebuilding efforts is at the heart of addressing the main drivers of conflict, as integral – and not additional – to the professionalization and capacity development of security forces.

This requires an understanding of "military civics" as an operational as well as strategic imperative. Like peace-building, which is another form of applied national strategy, it is as much a process from the bottom up as the top down. A key way to build confidence in, as well as the capacity of, security forces is in-depth leadership education training on military subordination to civilian rule and for military support of civil dialogue and reconciliation at community levels, as well as the designation, education, and training of civil-military specialists. It is no coincidence that the countries with the most robust civil-military capabilities in their armed forces are also among the world's leading democracies.

Moreover, inculcating a public service ethic among junior as well as senior police, paramilitary, and military leaders as integral to their professional code, for example, helps temper poor behavior and improve the civil-military relationship over time. Operational sensitization to civil-military imperatives at especially junior levels of command engenders long-term strategic payoffs since these leaders mature and translate operational understanding into political-military sensitivity. It improves operational effectiveness in these largely human security environments, helps mitigate drivers of conflict, and helps reduce corresponding threats. Research by military scholars Stephen Biddle and Stephen Long concludes that democracies are unusually successful in war due to superior human capital, harmonious civil-military relations, and moral imperatives, among other factors.[36]

This is where one aspect of Huntington's seminal study of civil-military relations is constructive: military institutions of any society are shaped by two forces. First, a functional imperative stemming from the threats to society's security and a societal imperative rising from the social forces, ideologies, and second, institutions dominant within the society. Military institutions that reflect only social values may be incapable of performing effectively their military functions. On the other hand, it may be impossible to contain within the society military institutions shaped purely by functional imperatives. The interaction of these two forces is the nub of the problem of civil-military relations.[37]

What the current imbalances in civil-military coordination and the balance and alignment of soft and hard power say is that there has been too much emphasis on the functional imperative in an era when the societal imperative is more appropriate. What they also say is that, as in civil-military relations, strategically driven civil-military coordination is managing the tensions between those two imperatives. Thus, civil-military coordination in practice (in whatever form or institutional point of reference) is mainly about two things: First, managing the relationship and interaction between civilian and military actors that maximizes the comparative advantages of these actors as they apply to the situation. Second, enabling and supporting the process of transition to peace, stability, and self-sustained development along civil-military lines, with the aims of "civilianizing" external assistance and "localizing" essential internal public services and governance functions.

Civil-military coordination is thus in good part a strategic management function—employing a risk-reward structure as soft and hard power are carrot and stick. As the private sector has learned: what accounted for fundamental shifts in longer term advantage was not operational-level innovation. It wasn't technology or product innovation, or new business models, or a new way of thinking about the whole industry. Again and again, it was management innovation—breakthroughs in how to organize and mobilize human capabilities.[38]

Given the nub of civil-military relations, the basic management functions of civil-military coordination, and a more global and strategic understanding of civil-military coordination in an environment mostly in human security terms, it becomes clear that civil-military coordination is not just a matter of linking strategy and tactics, security with development, and hard and soft power. It's a matter of how to organize and mobilize human capabilities.

In other words, civil-military coordination is a form of adaptive leadership: invoking both horizontal and vertical forms. In essence, civil-military coordination is thinking globally and acting locally—in military terms, thinking strategically at the operational and tactical levels. It employs a compass and not a cookbook, more a mindset than a skill set that operates from principles rather than prescriptions.[39] Adaptive leadership invokes a horizontal, collaborative, or strategic style of leadership found largely in civilian and non-state entities and characterized by persuasion versus a vertical, command-and-control, or tactical style of leadership found more in state structures such as the military and characterized by coercion.

Civil-military coordination is inherently comprehensive and collaborative. It leverages all forms of power and inflections of influence at all levels in order to create conditions for transition if not transformation. In doing so, it keeps hard power more implied than applied at best; or at worst, minimizes or mitigates its costs and risks when it must be applied. Synergistic and innovative, it enables, moderates, and balances, promoting unity of purpose and economy of effort while managing change, risk, and expectations.

Civil-military coordination is inherently socio-cultural. As a human enterprise, it is in essence about relationship-building, which is how things get done in human security environments. Because it involves engagement of the local populace, it demands cultural awareness, helping the credibility and legitimacy of the whole effort. By enabling a more proactive use of civilian and soft power, it elicits the military principle of offense. By enabling more effective leveraging of less costly and more sustainable civilian power over more costly and risk-laden hard power, it evokes the military principle of economy-of-force (or economy of effort, cost, and risk).

Civil-military coordination is anticipatory (and less reactive) due to the need to collaborate in advance in order to reach desired common objectives or manage disparate interests. As Hall of Famer Wayne Gretzky observed: "A good hockey player plays where the puck is. A great hockey player plays where the puck is going to be." Finally, it is adaptive and co-creative, more characteristic of learning organizations,[40] as it is inherently a learning activity, constantly conscious of situation and environment.

This understanding of civil-military coordination is not only incumbent upon military actors in security assistance. Civilian agencies of diplomacy and development, and NGOs and other civil society organizations, must in turn recognize that military organizations, for better or worse, are themselves extensions of civil society and thus have a role in making peace, albeit more indirect than direct. More pragmatically, it facilitates an eventual relationship with indigenous military, paramilitary and police forces and encourages them to maintain an appropriate balance between Huntington's imperatives in their own security sector, having seen that example in foreign forces. Beyond helping external militaries work themselves of their jobs, it helps for a more sustainable security sector reform process and a more secure and stable environment for both the civil society organizations and the emerging government institutions long after those forces leave.

Thus, both kinds of entities need to employ a qualitative blend of realism and idealism, respecting and accommodating, as best as possible, particular principles and equities. This can only come through establishing relationships, dialogue, and even rule-sets for operational civil-military interaction in order to learn about comparative advantages as well as limitations: CSOs generally take a long-term, relationship-based approach to development. Because of security, political and economic pressures, US government and military officials often attempt shorter-term, quick-impact development. The challenge is to design short-term programming that contributes toward long-term goals and to design long-term programming that supports short-term objectives. Addressing the contradictions in timeframes requires more extensive discussion between CSOs and ISAF policymakers.[41]

Another insight thus comes into play about what to do in the "steady state" at the strategic level. It is what is drawn upon during crisis response operations or in the field in general, with corresponding levels of success or failure. This critical strategic and operational capital— beneficial to both sides—is, at best, difficult to obtain once the operation begins. This is one among many lessons that never seem to get learned.

THE AMERICAN CIVIL-MILITARY METAPHOR

The threats, challenges, and opportunities of the changed environment of the 21st century are actually good news for the United States, for no other nation is better suited to lead this transformation of both national strategy and international leadership. Despite the incongruities of its current collective psychology, the foundation of American strength goes beyond its material wealth, its geography, or even its dynamic, multicultural civil society sourced by immigration and assimilation, along with its democratic national values—all of which represent tremendous strategic capital. The foundation of the strength of the United States has always been in the basis of its national narrative, in *e pluribus unum*.

This is, as Dr. Maan observed, "a metaphor that encompasses conflict. The US already has the advantage here; we *are* the alternative metaphor." The inherent advantage over fundamentalist or the competing narratives of vertically based, authoritarian powers such as China and Russia is that the original American narrative "has been one of inclusion . . . The United States does not have one narrative theme that must integrate or silence multiplicity . . . Our national narrative should not reflect singularity, but rather, coexistent multiplicity."[42]

In terms of its engagement with the world, the principles by which the United States governs its foreign relations is clearly depicted in a symbol more than two centuries old – namely, the obverse of the Great Seal of the

United States. The state, symbolized by the eagle, aspires for peace and civil society, looking in the direction of the olive branches in one talon while holding the arrows of war in reserve (or support) in the other.[43]

The Great Seal elegantly illustrates the balance and alignment as well as the application of national strength and power. "War and peace," after all, "remains the central dichotomy of national strategy."[44] It explains not only that the ultimate aim of American foreign and security policy is peace, but that peace has priority over security; that diplomacy and development takes precedence over defense, which is a last resort. It also shows that the objective of the use of force is, as every military philosopher from Sun Tzu to Colin Gray has stressed, is a better peace. And everyone, in turn, from Spinoza to Martin Luther King Jr., Ronald Reagan, and the Dalai Lama have pointed out that peace is not merely the absence of war and conflict, adding other qualifiers, among them justice and social harmony—which makes peace, as much as security—a process as much as an end state. But although peace without security is meaningless and unsustainable, which the symbol also implies, hard power is best and most effective when its implied rather applied.

The Great Seal's obverse also described the national strategic decision-making process when it comes to the use of force, which must be decided upon by the body politic and the nation as a whole. It also clearly depicts that military (or hard) power is subordinate to and supportive of civilian (or soft) power. In other words, this is the democratic civil-military relationship at all levels of application. This ethos must permeate not just policy, but its practice, in every aspect.

It will take years for the United States to get its own house in order in reestablishing a more authentic state of affairs in its civil-military relationship. There is greater impetus for this kind of transformation, not only from the strategic imperatives observed abroad, but from the American people themselves. In a remarkable study conducted by the Fund for Peace involving scores of town hall type meetings around the United States over two years, a major conclusion was while Americans still expected the United States to maintain its global leadership role, "It leads best when it's true to its values and when it works with others." The study also concluded:

> . . . there was remarkable consistency that America must lead in the world—but it leads most effectively when it "walks the talk" . . . how America leads is as important as whether it leads . . . Reorienting American policy priorities not only would enhance US global leadership, but was seen as yielding lasting influence . . . America was a stronger nation when it listened to people, and indeed, could learn from different countries, cultures, and experiences . . . Finally, there was significant discussion in most forums about the differences between "American power" and "national strengths." Many participants associated the former with an emphasis on coercive behavior in the world, while

they viewed the latter as concerning principles and values, such as democracy, liberty, and tolerance. While coercive means might be necessary in some cases, an over-reliance on them was seen as counter-productive and even disastrous; whereas pursuing policies on the basis of the nation's strengths was seen as the most effective way to produce lasting influence in the world.[45]

While the perils of the 21st century are coming more or less on their own, the promises emerging from the same paradigm are not as such. This calls for greater, not less, American international leadership:

> There was nothing inevitable about the world that was created after World War II. No divine providence or unfolding Hegelian dialectic required the triumph of democracy and capitalism, and there is no guarantee that their success will outlast the powerful nations that have fought for them. The ancient democracies of Greece and the republics of Rome and Venice all fell to more powerful forces or through their own failings. The evolving liberal economic order of Europe collapsed in the 1920s and 1930s. The better idea doesn't have to win just because it is a better idea. It requires great powers to champion it.[46]

Moreover, in every facet, it must be demonstrated in every facet visible to partner nations, doing more ourselves what we want others to do. There is nothing more powerful and enduring than leadership by example. This helps to close the say-do gap that has bedeviled especially American applied foreign and national security policy for decades. Practicing at home what you preach abroad evokes an age-old truism that Harry S. Truman applied in his message to Congress that launched the civil rights movement and concluded: "If we wish to inspire the peoples of the world whose freedom is in jeopardy, if we wish to restore hope to those who have already lost their civil liberties, if we wish to fulfill the promise that is ours, we must correct the remaining imperfections in our practice of democracy. We know the way. We need only the will."[47]

Reducing the narrative image of US domination and strong-arming facilitates internationalizing the overall effort, thus giving it greater cumulative power, persuasiveness, and influence and making it much more difficult to counter. Over there and over here being more inextricably connected than ever, it also helps promote a democratic culture, at home as well as abroad, in which the military is part of—not separate from—civil society:

> Democratic military professionals do not pursue their responsibilities to the state in isolation. They are part of a broader national security community comprised of national security professionals from both the civilian and military spheres, other actors such as journalists and academics who contribute intellectual capital and foster debate, legislative bodies with constitutional responsibilities to oversee and provide resources for national security policy,

and, finally, the public at large to whom all of the above are ultimately responsible.[48]

While this all portends is a more humble, collaborative, and demonstrative form of American leadership, it also means managing expectations—ours as well as theirs. "Thinking is easy," Goethe once said, "acting is difficult, and to put one's thoughts into action is the most difficult thing in the world." There is no paradigm shift, after all, until it reflects in programs, budgets, and operations—not just in speeches and policy papers. The walk must equal the talk.

If we are witnessing what Fareed Zakaria has called "the democratization of violence" and war, then the necessary antidote is the democratization of governance and peace. Winning the peace-wars of the 21st century takes time, patience, and a long, broad view in action: applied national strategy that is thinking globally and acting locally. Moreover, it takes looking beyond our power paradigm to see the strength of a national identity predicated on American values. Our approaches should reflect more of what we're about than what we're afraid of, right more than might. We need not look very far to see how to do this. Each of us carries it in our pockets and purses, on the back of a dollar bill. The eagle is already showing us the way.

NOTES

1. Department of Defense, *Decade of War, Volume I—Enduring Lessons from the Past Decade of Operations, Joint and Coalition Operational Analysis*, Joint Staff J7, (Washington, D.C.: DOD, 15 June 2012).

2. David Rothkopf, "Declaring an End to the Decade of Fear," *Foreign Policy*, 1 August 2013.

3. Christopher Holshek, "Ending Wars," *Diplomatic Courier*, 2 August 2012.

4. Nadia Schadlow, "Peace and War: The Space Between," *War on the Rocks*, 18 August 2014.

5. Russell F. Weigley, *The American Way of War* (Bloomington: Indiana University Press, 1973).

6. Christopher Holshek, "America's Foreign Engagement Gap," *The Huffington Post*, 4 March 2016.

7. Christopher Holshek, "National Security Über *Alles?*" *The Huffington Post*, 20 June 2013.

8. The author uses the term "civil-military coordination" in this paper not as an operational or doctrinal term, but rather in a much larger, grand strategic sense that includes the coordination of civilian-based and military power and influence at the strategic, operational, and tactical levels

9. Ajit Maan, *Counter-Terrorism: National Narratives* (Lanham: University Press of America, 2014).

10. The United Nations Development Programme's 1994 *Human Development Report* is considered a cornerstone publication for defining "human security" as including economic security, food security, health security, environmental security, personal security, community security, and political security as its main components – precisely how most underdeveloped nations, particularly, in Africa define "security" for them writ large. See Mahbub ul Haq, et al.,

Human Development Report 1994, United Nations Development Programme, Oxford University Press, Oxford, 1994.

11. Fukiyama is quoted in Thomas L. Friedman, "ISIS, Boko Harem, and Batman," *The New York Times*, 4 October 2014.

12. "Africa's Great Deficit: Challenges of Infrastructure Decay, Development," Center for Media Peace Initiatives, 3 June 2013.

13. David Weiss, "Syria: Refugee Communities and Redrawing the Map of the Middle East," *The Huffington Post*, 22 August 2014.

14. See the "Syria Crisis" home page, UN Office for the Coordination of Humanitarian Affairs.

15. Fareed Zakaria, "How long will America ignore Syria's suffering?" *The Washington Post*, 2 June 2016.

16. Eliza Griswold, "Can General Linder's Special Operations Forces Stop the Next Terrorist Threat?" *The New York Times*, 13 June 2014.

17. Christopher Holshek, "People Power," *Foreign Policy*, 10 July 2014.

18. Anthony H. Cordesman, "Key Factors Explaining the President's Islamic State Speech," Center for Strategic and International Studies, 9 September 2014.

19. Arthur K. Cebrowski, "Transformation and the Changing Character of War," ROA National Security Report, *The Officer* 55, July/August 2004.

20. David Rothkopf, "The Enemy Within", *Foreign Policy*, May-June 2012. See also Christopher Holshek, "The Enemies We Love," *The Huffington Post*, 4 May 2012.

21. Steven Metz, "For US, a Clear and Present Danger: Hyper-Partisanship," *World Politics Review*, 4 December 2016.

22. Diane Ohlbaum, "Shouldn't Security Rest on More than Blind Faith?" *The Hill*, 5 January 2016.

23. Rosa Brooks, "America's Police Problem Isn't Just About Police," *Foreign Policy*, 5 January 2016.

24. Richard H. Kohn, "The Constitution and National Security: The Intent of the Framers," in *The United States Military Under the Constitution of the United States* ed. Richard H. Kohn (New York: New York University Press, 1991), 87.

25. Marybeth Peterson-Ulrich, "Infusing Normative Civil-Military Relations Principles in the Officer Corps," in *The Future of the Army Profession*, ed. Don M. Snider and Lloyd J. Matthews, (New York: McGraw Hill, 2005), 655.

26. Robert D. Kaplan, "Looking the World in the Eye," *Atlantic Monthly*, December 2001, 70-72 Huntington published *The Soldier and the State* while an assistant professor of government at Harvard. The book was initially dismissed as propagandist by skeptical academics, and so infuriated his colleagues that they voted to deny him tenure two years later. Forced to leave, he joined the faculty at the University of Chicago. In 1962, Harvard realized its mistake and lured him back as a full professor. Students on campus staged protests during his classes, so his graduate students organized details to patrol the halls so lectures could proceed. Huntington continued teaching at Harvard for the next four decades, twice chairing the same department that once rejected him.

27. Suzanne C. Nielson and Don M. Snider (eds.) *American Civil-Military Relations: The Soldier and the State in a New Era*, (Baltimore: Johns Hopkins University Press, 2009), 387.

28. Suzanne C. Nielson, "American Civil–Military Relations Today: The Continuing Relevance of Samuel P. Huntington's *The Soldier and The State*," *International Affairs* 88: 2 (2012), 372-3.

29. Barack Obama, "The 2012 State of the Union," 25 January 2012.

30. Christopher Holshek, *Travels with Harley–Journeys in Search of Personal and National Identity*, (San Francisco: Inkshares, 2016), 63.

31. Phil Klay, "The Citizen-Soldier–Moral Risk and the Modern Military," The Brookings Institution, 24 May 2016.

32. Christopher Holshek, "A Country Worth Their Sacrifice," *The Huffington Post*, 26 May 2016.

33. *Irregular Enemies and the Essence of Strategy: Can the American Way of War Adapt?* (Carlisle, PA: US Army Strategic Studies Institute), March 2006, 5.

34. Frederik Rosen, "Third-generation Civil-Military Relations: Moving Beyond the Security-Development Nexus," *Prism* Vol. 2, No. 1, (December 2010), 28.

35. Stephen M. Walt, "Top 10 Lessons of the Iraq War," *Foreign Policy*, 12 March 2012.

36. Stephen Biddle and Stephen Long, "Democracy and Military Effectiveness–A Deeper Look," Journal of Conflict Resolution Vol. 48, No. 4, (August 2004), 525-546.

37. Samuel P. Huntington, *The Soldier and the State*, (Cambridge: Harvard Press, 1985), 2.

38. Gary Hamel, "Management Must Be Reinvented," World Innovation Forum, (2008).

39. For a more detailed discussion of the strategic nature of civil affairs and civil-military operations, see the author's "Civil-Military Power and the Future of Civil Affairs," Reserve Officer Association National Security Report, *The Officer*, May 2007, 45-48. The full version, based on an Army War College strategic research project, appeared as "The Scroll and the Sword: Synergizing Civil-Military Power," *Cornwallis Group XI: Analysis for Civil-Military Transitions*, (Nova Scotia: George Mason University–Pearson Peacekeeping Center, 2007).

40. For a greater understanding of the term "learning organization" in application, for a military perspective with respect to counterinsurgency operations, see John A. Nagl, *Learning to Eat Soup with a Knife*, (Chicago: University of Chicago Press, 2005); or, for a civilian bureaucratic perspective, see Thorsten Benner, Stephan Mergenthaler, Philipp Rotmann, *The Evolution of Organization Learning in UN Peace Operations Bureaucracy*, (Berlin: Global Public Policy Institute, 2011).

41. Lisa Schirch, "The Civil Society-Military Relationship in Afghanistan," *Peacebrief* 58, (United States Institute of Peace, Washington, D.C., 24 September 2010), 4.

42. Maan, 72-3.

43. For a detailed explanation of the Great Seal of the United States, see Joseph Campbell with Bill Moyers, *The Power of Myth*, (New York: Anchor Books, 1991), 31-34

44. For more on this discussion of peace and security in national strategy, see Christopher Holshek and Melanie Greenberg, "Toward a New Strategy of Peace," in the Department of Defense White Volume, *Socio-Cultural Analysis with the Reconnaissance, Surveillance, and Intelligence Paradigm*, Dr. Charles Eschlaeger (eds.), (July 2014), 1-11

45. Will Ferroggiaro, *The Use & Purpose of American Power in the 21st Century–Perspectives of Americans from the 2008-2009 National Dialogue Forums*, (Washington, DC: The Fund for Peace, June 2010), 15-16 and 32.

46. Robert Kagan, "Why the World Needs America," *The Wall Street Journal*, 11 February 2012.

47. Harry. S. Truman, "Special Message to the Congress on Civil Rights," 2 February 1948, Harry S. Truman Library & Museum.

48. Marybeth Peterson-Ulrich, "Infusing Normative Civil-Military Relations Principles in the Officer Corps," *The Future of the Army Profession*, 2nd Ed., Don M. Snider and Lloyd J. Matthews, eds., (New York: McGraw Hill, 2005), 656.

Chapter Five

Committed Service

*Bringing Together Service and Self-Fulfillment
for the Military Leader*

Christopher Mayer

American military services all value and advocate some form of selflessness. This attribute is emphasized as an essential component of leadership,[1] as military leaders are expected to put organizational mission and subordinates' welfare before their own. Despite reference to selflessness as part of the foundation of a service ethos, selflessness as a requirement for military leaders is not fully developed within the military's literature and has not received an adequate examination or critique. When a fully developed version of selflessness that adheres to the literal meaning of selflessness is examined closely, it becomes clear that this concept—which I will refer to as military selflessness (MS)—possesses weaknesses and that most military services do not completely embrace its essential elements. The problem, however, is that the military services' description of selflessness is not nuanced enough to distinguish from MS. Thus, there is conceptual ambiguity with how the military services articulate selflessness, leaving open the possibility that MS is the preferred view and that we ought to evaluate military leaders according to this standard. Military selflessness has attributes that are essential to military service, yet there is much about MS that should be rejected.

Adhering to MS risks undermining individuals' commitment to their organization and to their duties, and it potentially creates a gap between their role as military leaders and their other commitments and roles. It creates an unnecessary tension between the goals and interests individuals possess as military leaders and any other goals or interests they possess; it separates the person from his role as a military leader. Thus, it is important to explore what

97

military services mean by selflessness and what is the most appropriate service ethos for the military. In this chapter I examine MS to highlight some of its weaknesses. I then seek to extract the essential elements of MS needed for military service and integrate them with a different service called Committed Service, which, I argue, avoids some of the weaknesses of MS and provides a better, more precise, and more authentic service ethos for military leaders.

DEFINING MILITARY SELFLESSNESS

Two definitions of selflessness, taken from outside of the military context, highlight its essence. One definition proposes that being selfless means: "Having no regard for or thought of self; not self-centred; unselfish."[2] Another suggests that being selfless requires being "devoted to others' welfare or interest and not one's own."[3] Lack of selfishness is a component of both of the definitions; they both emphasize the outward-looking nature associated with selflessness and the ignoring of the self. Both definitions seem to suggest that if a person is focused exclusively on his or her self it undermines the possibility of being selfless. The focus should be on others. There are some significant differences between the two definitions and some ambiguity within the second. The first part of the first definition suggests that you should never think of yourself, while the second part mentions not being self-centered or selfish. Not being self-centered or selfish is much less demanding than having no regard for or thought of self. You can achieve the second part of this definition without achieving the first. Conversely, the second definition ambiguously uses "devoted." Does devoted mean not focused at all on one's self, or does it mean that you are mostly focused on others' welfare and interest? For the purpose of this chapter, we associate MS with the more demanding version of selflessness.

The military services' conception of selflessness meets the general approach of the above definitions with varying degrees of subordination of personal concerns. The Army employs the term selfless service as one of its Army Values and requires its members to "put the welfare of the Nation, the Army, and subordinates before your own. The needs of the Army and the Nation should come first."[4] The Air Force uses similar terminology when it describes its core value of "service before self," which requires Air Force personnel to accept the idea that, "professional duties take precedence over personal desires," requiring "a high level of professional skill, a 24-hour a day commitment, and a willingness to make personal sacrifices."[5] For the Marine Corps, selflessness requires "Marines [to] take care of their subordinates, their families, [and] their fellow Marines before themselves. The welfare of our country and our Corps is more important than our individual welfare."[6] The Navy's conception of selflessness is contained within its description of courage, and it urges Navy personnel to "make decisions in the best interest of the Navy and the nation, without regard to personal consequences."[7] Although not presented as explicitly as in the other services' literature, the Coast Guard's core values express the ideal of MS by proposing that members of the Coast Guard must be "committed to the successful achievement of our organizational goals."[8] The document also proposes, "We [the Coast Guard and its members] exist to serve," suggesting that the fundamental function of the Coast Guard's members is to serve the nation and the organization.[9]

Other nations' militaries also include selflessness in their statements of values. For example, in a Canadian military document it is written: "The profession of arms is distinguished by the concept of service before self, the lawful, ordered application of military force, and the acceptance of the concept of unlimited liability."[10] [11] The British Army employs the term "selfless commitment," which is, "reflected in the wording of the Oath of Allegiance which is taken on attestation. In it, soldiers agree to subordinate their own interests to those of the unit , Army, and Nation, as represented by the Crown." [12] It is these sorts of statements that form the basis for the conception of MS that I develop below. As noted above, I will align MS with the more demanding version of selflessness, even though military conceptions of selflessness vary in their demandingness.

From the service conceptions of selflessness and the dictionary definitions, I will characterize MS as follows: military selflessness is a character trait or disposition that military leaders should possess that makes them disposed, motivated, and able to place and promote the interests of nation and organization ahead of their personal interests (when the two conflict), regardless of the cost and sacrifice involved. Leaders' focus should be on promoting national and organizational interests, with no concern for their self-interest.

A selfless act in the military context is one in which military members intend to promote the interests of nation and organization without concern for their own interests. That is, the action is performed for the purpose of promoting national and organizational interests, without any thought being given to concerns of the self or, if there is, this concern plays no role in the final decision to perform the action. This distinction between the professional and personal self—and the tension that it produces—is problematic.

Good examples of what appear as MS can be found by examining the actions of Medal of Honor winners. Sergeant First Class Paul Smith (US Army), who was awarded the Medal of Honor, performed a selfless act by manning a machine gun to singlehandedly defeat an attack by a large number of Iraqi soldiers during the opening weeks of Operation Iraqi Freedom. He was able to stop the attack and protect his own soldiers, yet he died from the numerous wounds he received.[13] Given the overwhelming numbers of enemy soldiers attacking his platoon's position, Smith knew that there was a high probability that he would be killed, however, because he was a selfless leader, he manned the machine gun to protect those he was responsible for leading, in spite of the risk to himself.

Another example is Medal of Honor winner Sergeant First Class Jared Monti, who died trying to save one of his wounded soldiers caught between Monti's unit and the enemy. Monti made three attempts under heavy fire to rescue the soldier, dying on the last attempt. As with Smith, Monti knew that it was likely that he would die in the attempt to save the soldier, yet he did it anyway.[14] These sorts of examples are paradigmatic examples of MS, but there are other less heroic examples, discussed later, that demonstrate how MS can be applied during less dangerous circumstances.

A CRITIQUE OF MILITARY SELFLESSNESS

The conception of selflessness reflected in MS has many positive qualities. Selflessness as an ethos of service has served the military well in many respects. There are, however, issues with its compatibility with other qualities valued by the military compared to what we take to be a worthwhile and we see as ideals. It is these issues that lead me to propose a different service ethos (Committed Service) that incorporates aspects of MS but also accommodates other qualities valued by the military and resolves some of the tension between personal and professional commitments found in MS.

First, if the idea of selflessness is taken literally—as it is in MS—the military leader's role responsibilities are given absolute and permanent priority over personal commitments and interests. This raises worries similar to Susan Wolf's concerns about moral saints. Wolf[15] defines a moral saint as "a person whose every action is as morally good as possible, a person, that is, who is as morally worthy as can be."[16] The moral saint is disposed to be as moral as possible and always seeks to perform the action with the most moral worth, even if this means neglecting or ignoring other areas of his life. What is most important to this person, and what comes to dominate his deliberation and concerns, is performing the most morally worthwhile action possible. Wolf believes that conceptions of this sort of moral sainthood are not "compelling personal ideals,"[17] that they are not necessarily praiseworthy, and that we should not view moral saints as exemplars.

For Wolf, the problem of moral sainthood is that the saint is too focused on being moral; there is no time for anything else or for developing any other character traits that make us human. She suggests "moral virtues, all present in the same individual, and to an extreme degree, are apt to crowd out the nonmoral virtues, as well as many of the interests and personal characteristics that we generally think contribute to a healthy, well rounded, richly developed character."[18] At the very least, the moral saint is "too good for his own well-being," because he is living a life that is too focused on promoting good.[19] There is no room for hobbies because the moral saint "is devoting all his time to feeding the hungry or healing the sick or raising money for Oxfam."[20]

It is clear that military organizations do not desire their members to become moral saints. They support families and provide time off for members to engage in personal endeavors. Conceptually, if a military leader strictly adhered to MS, s/he would devote all of his/her energy and time to fulfilling his/her military role responsibilities or to developing his/her ability to fulfill his/her military role responsibilities. This makes her even more narrowly focused than Wolf's moral saint, who has a broader moral mandate that just professional obligations. This literal interpretation of MS makes it too demanding as a service ethos. Because of its over-demanding nature, it is important to clarify what the services need to get from a conception of selflessness and what needs to be removed.

A second weakness associated with MS concerns its focus on self-denial: it seems to separate fulfillment of the military leader's role responsibilities from his or herself. It suggests that one's identity as a military leader and one's performance of duties is not personal, not part of the self. That is, according to MS the leader who demonstrates self-denial is exemplary. Viewing service as self-denial, or viewing military responsibilities as separate from and with permanent priority over personal concerns, can be seen as limiting the extent to which military service can be seen as personally fulfilling and an essential part of one's identity.

What MS does not address well enough is that deriving personal satisfaction from fulfilling the role of military leader is acceptable and it is desirable to view service as an essential part of self that is integrated with one's identity. Certain elements of MS needs to be brought together with the idea that achieving fulfillment from military service as a leader and integrating service with self are valuable and ideal. Also that self-fulfillment and incorporating one's military role into one's identity is not the same as selfishness or as an excessive focus on personal interests. Linking self fulfillment to the fulfillment of the military leader's role is possible and, when combined with some of the ideas of MS, actually strengthens the leader's commitment to his/her role and subordinates, as well as the institution that s/he serves.

Despite the primacy of concern for nation and service that should dominate the focus of the leader, the literature grants that military leaders will experience conflict, accepting that most will resemble Aristotle's continent person rather than the virtuous person.[21] Never able to be free from the inclination to promote desires and goals associated with other roles, MS suggests that military leaders will necessarily struggle to suppress desires to pursue interests and obligations outside of the military role. Thus, they must develop the ability to subordinate and submerge other desires and commit-ments that necessarily compete with their commitment to military service.

Given what is written in the literature and the very meaning of the term selflessness, this conflict appears to be between the member's two selves (military versus nonmilitary), rather than an internal struggle between sets of interests or desires. The military member occupies a role that constitutes a separate self or identity, with clearly prescribed responsibilities; s/he should not allow desires of the nonmilitary self to interfere with fulfillment of these responsibilities. This is why the leader who exemplifies MS is somewhat like Aristotle's continent person in that s/he faces continual conflict; in this case, however, it is a conflict between two selves. What s/he must do is to consis-tently act and selflessly approach military service by having the ability to suppress the desires of the nonmilitary self. While this conflict likely hap-pens for many, it should not be presented as an ideal because it neglects and undermines many of the attributes valued by the military. It portrays a pos-sibly endless and grinding tension that hinders the ability of the military leader to perform his or her role properly. Bringing together essential aspects of MS with another view provides a much stronger approach to service, which is committed service (CS). It is important to note that this in no way seeks to make light of the risk and sacrifice associated with military service. In fact, it makes the willing acceptance of these risks and sacrifices in the manner advocated by CS even more praiseworthy.

COMMITTED SERVICE

Committed service (CS) as a service ethos for military leaders can best be illustrated through examining a historical example. Although the example is taken from outside of the military, it demonstrates how a person can success-fully integrate his or her role responsibilities as a leader with his or herself and identity by viewing fulfillment of these responsibilities as self-fulfill-ment.[22] This makes for more authentic leadership, as the leader does not view self-denial as a necessary requirement for service as a leader. It also allows for a more integrated identity.

In *Lest Innocent Blood Be Shed: The Story of the Village of Le Chambon and How Goodness Happened There*, Philip Hallie describes how the people of Le Chambon, France, saved thousands of Jewish refugees (who were total strangers) from the Vichy French government and the Nazis. Andre Trocme was the protestant pastor of a church in Le Chambon and was the organizer and leader of the town's movement to help the refugees as they escaped the authorities. [23] While Trocme assumed tremendous risk in leading this effort, he does not approach his service as denial of the self or even as a sacrifice. Rather, in him we see a disposition to help others that is linked to his conception of self, making his service as a leader self-fulfilling and an affirmation of his values, which demonstrates some of the problems with MS.

As a pastor, Trocme looked to the Bible to see how he could successfully meet the requirements of his role. He also looked to the Bible to see how he should act as a person. The Bible guided Trocme's actions as well as the actions of the other villagers:

> But one part of those [Biblical] passages they [the villagers] were not willing to ignore was the statement of the Lord that if the innocent are slain in a city of refuge, the guilt of that bloodshed will be upon those who committed themselves to sheltering them in their city. The ministers—and the people they led—believed that they had a duty to protect the refugees, a duty that, if violated, would bring condemnation upon them as betrayers of a trust and of a commitment. [24]

Trocme saw helping those in need, in this case Jewish refugees, as a responsibility associated with the fact that he was a pastor who was obligated to adhere to Biblical principles. This involved personally helping the refugees and leading the village to do so as well. This constituted self-fulfillment on two levels. First, Trocme cared a great deal about doing well in his role: he recognized its importance and his view of himself as a person was dependent on how well he occupied the role of pastor. Consequently, he sought to protect the refugees and accepted risk, because to do so was to successfully fulfill the role of pastor, which is something that was personally important to him. He was also a Christian who was deeply invested in living the way the Bible guided him to live, which included viewing himself as a member of a common humanity responsible for helping all humans. Therefore, when he occupied his role well he was not only flourishing as a pastor, but also as a person. The values he promoted and character traits he exemplified as a pastor were the same as those he sought to promote and exemplify as a person, which made occupying the role of pastor well constitutive of Trocme's conception of a good life. The hard work he did as pastor was not an instance of self-denial but self-fulfillment and expression. It reflected an integration of his work as a leader with his living of a fulfilling life as a person.

Philosopher Neera Badhwar proposes that in the actions of the people of Le Chambon there is a type of "moral excellence, an intuitively recognizable excellence of character and action, which is at one a form of deep altruism and a form of self interest." [25] Badhwar goes on to say that the person who exemplifies this excellence is motivated by a type of self interest concerned with living a life that is well lived and deeply satisfying. [26] What Badhwar hopes to show is that this type of self interest is not only innocuous, but also adds moral value to the action as well as to the person who performs it.

Badhwar relies on the empirical research cited in "Altruism and the Theory of Rational Action: Rescuers of Jews in Nazi Europe" to eliminate many potential motives for the actions of those in Le Chambon (known as the Rescuers) who assisted the Jewish refugees. Based on the research they conducted, Monroe, Barton, and Klingemann[27] suggest that the Rescuers did not act to obtain monetary reward or praise to "feel good about themselves," to be the ones who rescued the Jews,[28] because of peer pressure,[29] or an abundance of resources.[30] Instead, they acted because of a true concern for the refugees, but also, and this is Badhwar's focus, because:

> Rescuers' interest in saving Jews expressed their sense of themselves as part of a common humanity, a sense that dominated their normally primary sense of themselves as parents, lovers, and friends. The thought of betraying this sense by refusing any help to the Jews would have been seen as an expression of weakness and the contemplated act as an act of self-betrayal. And the thought of undergoing an identity shift as the result of such an act of self betrayal would have been the thought of an irreparable loss—a loss of self.[31]

Badhwar is suggesting that because the Rescuers' sense of self was integrated with their desire and commitment to being part of a common humanity, their actions were not self-interested due to a desire for glory or to maintain their reputation in the community. Instead, they were self-interested because their personal identity was linked to promoting the interests of a common humanity. To not promote these interests when the opportunity clearly presented itself would have been personally damaging.

We see Trocme demonstrating this concern for humanity as a person and in his role as a pastor. When the Jewish refugees began to arrive, fulfilling the role well for Trocme meant sheltering them himself, and leading the villagers to shelter them, because the refugees were innocent. He cared about fulfilling his role well because he cared about the refugees and because he was being true to himself. Performing his duties as a pastor allowed him to express values that were important to him and constituted self-fulfillment, even though performing them involved risk.

Badhwar concludes that Rescuers "had an interest in acting altruistically not only for the sake of affirming others, but also for the sake of affirming, and being true to, themselves."[32] She goes on to argue, "The presence of such [self-affirming] motivations may be indicative of the greater depth and strength of a person's altruistic motivations." If Trocme grudgingly led the villagers because his duties conflicted with his personal desires or commitments or his actions were separate from his self, his actions would still be admirable, but less so than his actual approach because it could be said (in the case of grudging performance of duty) that Trocme was not fully interested in helping others. As a leader he would possess conflicting dispositions: the disposition to help those in need in order to fulfill his role well versus the disposition to focus only on his own welfare. In this case, it could be said that while he possessed a disposition for altruistic behavior, it was not truly aligned with his other dispositions. In reality, Trocme felt no conflict at all as he was fully behind helping the refugees. As a leader he was being true to himself by fulfilling his responsibilities. He was more like Aristotle's virtuous person who is consistent with CS, rather than Aristotle's continent person who resembles MS.

Badhwar captures this connection of altruism and self interest when she writes, "it is because, and only because, Rescuers' altruistic values *were* thus central and they did have this self-interested motive for acting altruistically, that they could do so spontaneously, naturally and (in a literal sense) *whole-heartedly* i.e. from an *undivided* [emphasis added] sense of the desirable and the desired, and an undivided desire for their own good and others' good."[33] It can be said that Rescuers performed altruistic actions for others and for themselves, so that they could maintain their sense of self that was altruistic.

For Trocme, helping the Jewish refugees was something that he had to do because he occupied the role of pastor, viewed it in his interests (as a pastor and a person) to fulfill this role well, and desired to follow the example of Jesus. His assistance to the refugees fulfilled the responsibilities of his role, but it also allowed him to flourish as a person. To fail to help would have not only been a failure to fulfill his role properly, but would have also been to act against his own interests. He wholeheartedly led the villagers to help the refugees rather than with the type of struggle promoted by MS. Trocme's story demonstrates that a leader's service, even when involving extreme risk of the sort that selflessness is meant to address, can be brought even closer and integrated with the self rather than having to be separated from or representing a denial of self. This means that occupying the role of military leader can be seen self-fulfilling rather than self-denying.

To close this section it is helpful to return to a military example and consider it within the framework offered by the account of Trocme's actions. SFC Monti was the noncommissioned officer who risked and sacrificed his life to save one of his soldiers during operations in Afghanistan. His action here reflects his concern with fulfilling his role well. While the sort of heroic action that wins Medals of Honor is usually the type cited when examining service ideals, Monti's actions outside of combat confirm how he integrated his military role into his identity. While visiting one of his soldier's homes, he noticed that the soldier and his family did not have a kitchen table; his family had to sit on the floor to eat. This was unacceptable to Monti, so he went to his house and returned with his own kitchen table, which was worth $500. Monti would rather do without a table than see his soldier and family without a table. This concern for others can also be seen during deployments in Bosnia and Afghanistan, where he gave away packages from home to children so that they could have the clothes.[34]

Monti's actions reflect a desire to do well in his role as a military leader. Monti recognized the important of fulfilling his role well, and he did so with concern and compassion for those he led. As a member of the military, his professional identity was inextricably part of his sense of self: his identify was fully integrated. While his actions were altruistic and were sacrificial (his life, table, clothes), it is hard to call them selfless since they reflect the type of person Monti was. They, along with his Medal of Honor act, were acts of self-expression that he likely performed wholeheartedly: they were not suppressions of the self. This makes Monti even more admirable and the best sort of hero. He was committed to his role and to helping others, and this was as important to him as a person as it was to him as a military leader. His concern for others was not just an attribute he possesses as a military leader, but it was also one he possessed as a person.

COMMITTED SERVICE

Committed Service as a service ethos promotes integration of the military leader's role rather than the isolation of the self from this role. It reflects the importance of viewing service as self-fulfilling and identity conferring. Although it diverges from MS in some ways, CS still incorporates the aspects of MS that are necessarily linked to the military role, including its fundamental principles of focusing on promoting national and organizational interests and accepting the risks and consequences associated with occupying the demanding role of military leader in war and in peace.

The following excerpt from a letter captures the connection between self-fulfillment and service as a military leader that is an essential element of CS. The letter was written by Major John Alexander Hottell, an Army officer who led soldiers in Vietnam, in the event of his death, which occurred in 1970. Hottell wrote:

> I am writing my own obituary ... [because] I am quite simply the last authority on my own death. I love the Army: it reared me, it nurtured me, and it gave me the most satisfying years of my life. Thanks to it, I have lived an entire lifetime in 26 years. It is only fitting that I should die in its service. We all have but one death to spend, and insofar as it can have any meaning it finds it in the service of comrades in arms. And yet, I deny that I died FOR anything – not my Country, not my Army, not my fellow man, none of these things. I LIVED for these things, and the manner in which I chose to do it involved the very real chance that I would die in the execution of my duties. I knew this and accepted it, but my love for West Point and the Army was great enough—and the promise that I would someday be able to serve all the ideals that meant anything to me through it was great enough—for me to accept this possibility as a part of a price which must be paid for all things of great value. If there is nothing worth dying for—in this sense—there is nothing worth living for.[35]

Of this, Roger Nye comments that what Hottell demonstrated "was not 'selfless service' but 'self-in-service.'"[36] In the letter, Hottell suggests that he found meaning in service and lived for it. It was not something that he did grudgingly, nor a practice in self-denial though he knew that there was a good chance that he would die in Vietnam. Instead, it was something he did out of love; he was personally connected to the institutions and ideals that he served, and this was self-fulfilling for him rather than self denying. His comment that the Army reared and nurtured him suggests that occupying the military role allowed him to achieve self fulfillment by acquiring traits of character that he saw as worthy of a good life and that the possession and exercise of these traits allowed him to feel as though he lived an entire lifetime in 26 years. He also was serving ideals that "meant something to me," making it in his interest to promote them as a leader, both because they were objectively valuable, but also because they were personally important to him. Hottell demonstrates that military leaders can possess significant identity-conferring commitments other than occupation of the role of military leader and that this does not undermine commitment to the military role.

Hottell's letter captures much of what a service ethos should articulate regarding how military leaders ought to occupy their roles. One thing that it does very well is to connect occupation of the military leader role with self-fulfillment and integration of this role with the self and these ideas are distinguishing features of CS. The military's service ethos should not promote or accept perpetual conflict within a person or between their identities; it should also not promote denial of self but should aim for an integration of the member's role and her other commitments, leading to a unified identity and a view of occupying the role of military leader as completely compatible with leading and necessarily part of (for some) a fulfilling life. The leader should wholeheartedly act with consistent values and traits. The military seems to desire this sort of unified identify but the unexamined use of self-lessness as the basis for a service ethos puts this in jeopardy.

Offering CS as a new approach for the military's service ethos is not to imply a complete rejection of MS. For example, to fulfill their roles properly, military leaders will still have to perform risky actions and operate in life-threatening conditions. Additionally, the role of military leader is still demanding in peacetime. It requires a great deal of time and effort to meet the expectations that the profession requires. Thus, military leaders cannot be selfish or completely self-centered. Where I move away from MS is in terms of its character requirements and how the military leader approaches occupying her role. Currently, military literature contains many references to self-denial, self-sacrifice, and subordinating self as defining and desirable aspects of military leaders' approach to occupying their role. This is problematic because it does not recognize that viewing role occupation as a form of self-fulfillment and part of the member's identity can elicit a deeper dedication to the role and a more authentic and personal form of leadership. This is why CS, with elements of MS, is more appropriate than relying on MS. It reflects the personal commitment and dedication that military leaders should exemplify given the good that the military role promotes and the benefits it provides when people occupy the role well. It also demonstrates the consistency of character and integration of a person's life that the military should desire in its leaders.

It is fitting to end by returning to the example of Paul Smith. Smith's sister spoke of him during a speech in which she described one of many examples of her brother's commitment to his role as a military leader:

> Paul Ray had an incredible love for the troops under his command. One Christmas, the wife of a Soldier in Paul Ray's platoon had just had surgery and the Soldier and his wife were unable to provide a Christmas for their family. So, Paul Ray collected food from the company Christmas party, and he and Birgit bought presents for the children, and they took them to the Soldier's home. Paul Ray's family never heard of this until recounted to them by friends after his death.[37]

Like Monti, Smith's concern for those he led suggests that even though he made the ultimate sacrifice in Iraq, and a lesser one by buying Christmas presents for his soldiers' children, his actions were an expression of his self rather than a denial of it. He was personally committed and invested in his service as a leader, as demonstrated in dangerous and common situations, and he achieved self-fulfillment from this service, which makes him an exemplar of Committed Service.

NOTES

1. All military members are expected to be selfless; however, it is essential that military leaders exemplify this quality. If they do not, those they lead are much less likely to be selfless. My focus will be on leaders.

2. Oxford English Dictionary, "Selfless," Retrieved July 12, 2013.

3. On-line Etymology Dictionary, "Selfless," Retrieved July 12, 2013.

4. United States Army, *Army Leadership: Competent, Confident, and Agile (FM 6-22)*. (Washington D.C.: Headquarters Department of the Army, 2006).

5. United States Air Force. *Air Force Core Values*.

6. United States Marine Corps, *Marine Corps Values: A User's Guide for Discussion Leaders (MCRP 6-11B)*, (Washington, D.C.: Headquarters, United States Marine Corps, 1988).

7. United States Navy, *Navy Core Values*. Retrieved July 12, 2013.

8. United States Coast Guard, *Coast Guard Core Values*. Retrieved July 12, 2013.

9. Because of the message that the ethos of selflessness sends to military leaders, some worry that it promotes the idea that commanders should sleep very little or push themselves to exhaustion. See Jonathan Shay's *Ethical Standing for Commander Self-Care: The Need for Sleep* for a discussion of this phenomenon.

10. Canadian Forces Leadership Institute, *Duty With Honour: The Profession of Arms in Canada* (Chief Of Defence Staff by the Canadian Defence Academy: Canadian Forces Leadership Institute, 2009).

11. Unlimited liability is the idea that once someone occupies the military role, subject to its contractual terms which includes performing duties in dangerous environments where there is a high likelihood of serious injury or death.

12. British Army, *Values and Standards of the British Army* (2008).

13. United States Army, "Sergeant First Class Paul R. Smith: Medal of Honor-War on Terrorism."

14. United States Army, "Sergeant First Class Jared Monti: Medal of Honor-Operation Enduring Freedom."

15. Wolf, Susan, "Moral Saints," *The Journal of Philosophy* 79:8, (1982), 419-439.

16. Ibid, 419

17. Ibid, 419

18. Ibid, 420

19. Ibid, 421

20. Ibid, 421

21. The continent person knows what is right but struggles to do it, while the virtuous person knows what is right but does not struggle to do it. See Aristotle, *Nicomachean Ethics*, Book VII, chapter 9, for a discussion of the continent person.

22. I thank an anonymous review for pointing out that I should explain why

23. I thank Loren Lomasky for encouraging me to focus on Andre Trocme because he best illustrates the linkage of self-fulfillment to the fulfillment of one's role responsibilities. Trocme's wife and the other villagers do not occupy an official role in the way that Trocme does, which makes his case more relevant to military leaders.

24. Phillip P Hallie, *Lest Innocent Blood Be Shed*. (New York: Harper & Row, 1979).

25. Neera Kapur Badhwar, A"ltruism Versus Self-Interest: Sometimes a False Dichotomy," in Ellen Frankel Paul, Fred D. Miller, Jr. & Jeffrey Paul (Eds.), *Altruism,* (Cambridge: Cambridge University Press, 1993), 90-117.

26. Ibid, 93

27. Monroe, Kristen R., Michael C. Barton, & Ute Klingermann, "Altruism and the Theory of Rational Action: Rescuers of Jews in Nazi Europe," *Ethics* 101:1, (1990), 103-122.

28. Ibid, 109

29. Ibid, 113

30. Ibid, 115

31. Neera Kapur Badhwar, "Altruism Versus Self-Interest: Sometimes a False Dichotomy," in Ellen Frankel Paul, Fred D. Miller, Jr. & Jeffrey Paul (Eds.), Altruism, (Cambridge: Cambridge University Press, 1993), 90-117.

32. Ibid, 109

33. Ibid, 115

34. David Moore, "Jared Monti: Mortally Wounded Soldier Still Rescues Fallen Teammate," *Veterans United Network*, 20 July 2012.

35. Roger Nye "The Commander's Concept of Duty," In David McGurk (Ed.), *West Point's Perspectives on Officership*, (Boston: McGraw Hill Custom Publishing, 2005), 39-50.

36. Ibid, 80

37. United States Army. "Sergeant First Class Paul R. Smith," (2005).

Chapter Six

The *Muhajirat*

Tracing the Literature of Radical Women

Farhana Qazi

INTRODUCTION

Terrorism has always been a battle of ideas, reflecting a desire for immediate attention and change in the international world order. Like men, women leave their homes, families and communities to join terrorist organizations, such as The Islamic State in Iraq and Syria (ISIS), to support violent extremism. Because of their gender, women assume an auxiliary role within most male-oriented Islamist-based violent organizations and use a wide range of available technologies to market the capabilities and goals of the group they join. Female recruits have excelled at articulating a clear mission statement in support of ISIS and other groups, manipulating Islamic text in order to turn passive observers into active participants in violent extremism. Strategic communications allow radical women to shape the narrative of intolerance, perceived injustice, and hatred as well as express their grievances and audience perceptions of inequality to manipulate and influence vulnerable populations.

It is important to recognize that female recruits do not need to be trained to shape identities, relationships, and interactions among other women. It is assumed that the online network of female radicals nurture and perpetuate extremist messages and draw on their own compelling stories of anger, grief, trauma, isolation, rage, loss, and use other emotional indicators to guide the narrative of resistance that ISIS and other groups espouse against their enemies. Through writing, radical women are empowered and become integrated into a community of extremists while affirming their own self-image. For others, writing may be cathartic and serve as a way to resolve associated

111

symptoms of post-traumatic stress order, though more research in this area needs to be done to prove the hypothesis that *only* women with trauma write effectively.

Literature of radical women collected by the author for over a decade can help counter-terrorism experts, analysts and authorities understand the mindset and outlook of radical women. An examination of print and online material by radical women is the first step to creating a realistic counterterrorism policy and practice to defeat the powerful and persuasive messages in violent extremism.

This chapter explores the range of narrative identities of extremist women that is reflected in their writing. A study of women's literature considers their evolving life stories; how they have integrated the reconstructed past into their work; and ways radical women have imagined the future to provide them with hope, unity, and purpose. The life stories of radical women are featured in a plethora of online and print publications, and include redemptive meanings in suffering and adversity, which allow women false security and safety in the midst of conflict.

EMPOWERING WOMEN

The *muhajirat* (female migrants to terrorist groups) play an important role in extremist propaganda and radicalization. By relocating themselves into terrorist territory, radical women have reshaped and reinvigorated the online space of radicalization. These women contribute to online discussions to recruit, radicalize, and reaffirm their own identity as women willing to give up everything for martyrdom, marriage, and the men of violent extremism. Their sacrifice and struggles for violent extremism offer a false sense of empowerment.

Whether radical women achieve equality or empowerment through their involvement in violent extremism is not entirely clear, but evidence of women's participation in earlier armed struggles and nationalist causes proves that women's involvement has not significantly altered their social status within their respective societies. If women historically have little to gain from joining terrorist groups, then why are women eager and enthusiastic to join? Because no two women are alike, the answer to participation will vary.

Most radical women will never rise above the secondary role in male-driven terrorist organizations, although it can be argued that the women who write about violent jihad may believe their role as propagandists is self-affirming and rewarding. Other women may desire more than just *jihad bil qalam* (jihad of the pen): a spiritual concept that refers to the spread of Islam through education and training, not the perverse language of violence. Writing offers radical women an opportunity to make an individual contribution to the terrorist movement, which in itself can be rewarding.

For decades, women have been crafting messages of violence to reach a wider audience. Before social media, radical women published articles in magazines, newsletters, and pamphlets distributed widely to Muslim-majority communities to persuade, push and urge other men and women to join violent extremism. Today, new social media has made extremist messaging that much easier for radical women (and men). Evidence suggests that radical women use Facebook, Twitter, online chat rooms, and other social media accounts to contribute to extremist propaganda.

Drawing on earlier research and interviews of radical women, the author developed a framework to understand the motives for female participation in violence called the Four Rs: [1]

1. *Revenge* for the loss of family members, and/or loss of community/ nation;
2. *Respect* from the larger Muslim community for her sacrifice;
3. *Reassurance* that she is a capable and equal partner in jihad; and
4. *Recruitment* of other women to violent jihad to sustain the terror group

This list is not meant to exclude other factors that could inspire women to write in support of terrorists. Professor Andrew Silke has argued that certain factors exist within a given community that enables groups to employ martyrdom, for example. His argument assumes that some groups have a "cultural precedent for self-sacrifice; the conflict is long-running ... and involves casualties on both sides; and the protagonists are desperate."[2] In a separate article, Silke highlights the psychology of vengeance; social identification (i.e., the need to belong to a local or international community of believers); accessible entrée into a terrorist group; an elevated status and personal rewards; and the feeling of exclusion from mainstream society—all of which leave individuals vulnerable to religious indoctrination.[3]

Accepting that other motivations are likely, two factors offer women a heightened sense of awareness of the world in which they live: a breakdown of a woman's societal structures (including foremost the loss of her family and community) and increased opportunities for women to volunteer for or join terrorist groups. Through the latter, women—even those *not* living in war, occupation, or armed struggle—can become members of violent extremism. Scholars and psychiatrists refer to this as embracing a "collective identity."[4] For example, an American woman in Philadelphia, Colleen La-Rose, a.k.a. "Jihad Jane," indicated in 2008 on YouTube that she wanted to help the suffering Muslim people—a standard sentiment even among moderate/mainstream (non-violent) Muslims with a need to help Muslims in conflict. Other terrorism experts, namely Dr. Jerrold Post and Paul Horgan, explain the need to be part of a wider group by stressing the importance of the social psychological perspective as the "most powerful lens through which to examine and explain terrorist behavior."[5] Through the identification process, the mobilization of women into terrorist organizations represents an evolving network.[6]

While some rely on social science theories to explain the rise of female terrorism, it is far more challenging to define, describe and determine the role of ideology as a motivator for women's inclusion into religious-based organizations. As a principle, religion can be used to signify many things, including the *process* by which women join; a *consciousness* of belonging to a group; and a *social and political will* to realize the terrorists' end goal. However, in numerous lectures and publications, the author has argued that religious doctrine is an unlikely central motivator, even while religious language is a component of the narratives that radical women weave into their work.

It should be noted that Islam as a guiding doctrine offers symbols and signs for women—and men—to justify violent action and animosity towards those whom they are fighting against. According to Professor Mia Bloom, employing religious language to justify violent extremism does not detract from the terror organizations' pursuit of power. She writes, "Their political survival is ultimately more important than any ideology."[7] In a forthcoming book on radical Islam, the author examines religious text couched within the narrative of injustice used by women to convince her readers to take action.

As a sign of protest, radical women write to be seen. Their invisibility is exactly what enables them to grow their readership and engage with an online audience. In their print and online literature, women stress 4 Reasons to Protest, a model that complements the earlier 4Rs framework. *Prestige.* Women are as capable as men. Writing empowers radical women, who are given a voice and an opportunity to actively participate in violent extremism, thereby elevating their status as contributors to terrorism. *Protect.* Women write on behalf of their families, communities, and a network of men to ensure their survival. Women write for and about men. They celebrate the death of men in their literature, calling them martyrs and heroes, which protects the narrative of Heavenly rewards for those who make the ultimate sacrifice, or death. *Power.* The power of the pen cannot be understated. In writing, radical women can inflict damage on the enemy by drawing in male and female recruits to attack the enemy, thus strengthening and growing their membership. In writing, some radical women have shown to be persuasive and powerful—women can shame men with words as well as attract men and women to join their cause. *Peace.* Women demand an end to the conflict that they have vowed to join. Like men, women desire immediate political transformation and may hope for greater equal opportunities and rights, once the conflict is over. The 4Ps are not comprehensive, and there are likely other explanations that motivate radical women to write on behalf of a male-led terrorist organization.

As stated earlier, whether writing empowers women in a terrorist organization is yet to be proven. But women's literature shows that they *feel* they are engaged in meaningful work. Writing offers women a voice—they can speak out against "perceptions of persecution and feelings of cultural isolation."[8] They can encourage other Western-based Muslims and Muslims worldwide to join them in a cause worth fighting for by reposting images of "children who have been injured or killed in violent conflict, creating strong emotionally charged narratives."[9] Women reinterpret global events, showcasing human tragedy; highlighting the abuse of women by their enemies; and justifying violence as the *only* way to resolve the violent persecution of Muslim communities. With the approval and praise of their men, radical women glorify violent jihad with words while guarding their gender in a strict separation of the sexes. Therefore, they are able to conceal their identities from the mainstream media and the general public. As anonymous actors, using fake identities, these women may believe they are liberated to write, so long as they remain undetected, bypassing security but gaining worldwide attention.

Furthermore, these narratives often reflect radical women's experiences, both lived and imagined; their observations and a rewriting of cultural and religious norms; and often are a direct response to local and global grievances. With global communication systems, radical women know can convey, convince, and captivate vulnerable women *and* men, using the seductive power of persuasion and worldwide publicity on the Internet and in print media. This chapter includes a broad spectrum of radical women's writings, including the origins of their violent expression that predates the birth of al-Qaeda into the present-day ISIS propaganda, to reflect the different powerfully emotive themes that shape the narrative, with theological backing from former and current Islamic ideologues.

THE MEANING OF JIHAD

The word jihad is sacred to many Muslims, but is misinterpreted on all sides of the political spectrum.[10] The extremists' focus on a particular vision of Islam has given rise to a battle of belief and unbelief and sparked a war of words in which various groups and individuals are now reasserting their right to claim the true meaning of jihad. Discoloring its original intent and purpose, extremists are fighting for the unrelieved agony of the Muslim *umma* (community)—a point with some credibility even to "moderate" Muslims—but choose to satisfy their anger with narratives driven by revolutionary change in their society.

Contrary to popular Western myth, jihad has a broad semantic content, and is different from *qittal* (fighting). Both terms, jihad and *qittal,* have "significantly different meanings and uses in the Qur'an."[11] "The latter word involves killing and bloodshed, whereas jihad's original intent is to struggle to attain God's pleasure." Among the first Qur'ani verses for fighting is number twenty-two:

> Leave is given to those who fought because they were wronged—
> surely God is able to help them—who were expelled from their
> habitations without right, except that they say Our Lord is God.

To infer that jihad is synonymous with "holy war" is therefore inaccurate.[12] For the larger Muslim world, jihad is simply an everyday concept: an act of Islamic worship, [13] derived from the Arabic verb *jahada,* which means "effort and striving."[14] For believing Muslims, jihad is a living, breathing concept. Muslims strive to embrace good and reject evil. Even for secular, liberal (non-practicing Muslims), jihad is a positive term that reflects the inner struggle of one's life.

While there are many forms of jihad, all of which are defined by a set of rules, jihad is best described as self-defense: defense against temptation, defense against Satan, defense against the unjust, and (most commonly known in the West) defense against religious persecution.[15] In reality, the misappropriation of the idea into an "uncompromisingly belligerent interpretation of jihad."[16]

In the past, Muslim legal theorists have authorized the rights and duties of the Muslim scholar to include the declaration of war against a *kuffar* (infidel) ruler or people. Indian scholar Maulavi Chiragh Ali states that Muslims have an absolute right to fight in defense of Islam when it is attacked. Similar arguments have been circulated and repackaged in the works of Dr. Abdallah Azzam, the former veteran *mujahideen* coordinator of the Afghan jihad, and the writings of Yousef al-Iyiri, a key ideologue of the al Qaeda network in Saudi Arabia.

Since the start of the Afghan war, Azzam and other theologians in Saudi Arabia called for the return of the golden era of Islam by advocating defensive jihad. The mantle of jihad prevails throughout Azzam's writings, texts by the early Egyptian revolutionaries, and *fatwas* issued by Saudi-based clerics.

Jihad as *fard ayn,* or religious obligation, was first introduced in a *fatwa* written by Azzam in *The Defense of Muslim Lands*: "jihad becomes *fard ayn* [a global obligation] on every Muslim male and female." [17] No permission was needed from parents, husband, or a male guardian for women to wage jihad against the infidel (*kuffar*)—a consistent theme played in earlier and later works by Islamic reformists, theorists, and jihadis. Drawing on classical

Muslim scholars, Azzam quotes Ibn 'Abidin from the Hanafi school of thought in *Join the Caravan*:

Jihad is *fard 'ayn* when the enemy has attacked
Any of the Islamic heartland, at which point it
Becomes *fard 'ayn* on those close to the enemy... [18]

One of the leading female propagandists was Umm Mohammed, Azzam's wife. In an interview for the London-based newspaper, *Al-Sharq al-Awsat,* Umm Muhammad called herself the "mother figure," and coordinated among the wives of the mujahideen in Peshawar, a northern town in Pakistan.[19] In March 2003, the same woman told the same paper why she helped establish al-Qaeda's women wing: "The idea came from the success of martyr operations carried out by young Palestinian women in the occupied territories. Our organization is open to all Muslim women wanting to serve the [Islamic] nation." She warned the world that a new strike will "make America forget...the September 11 attacks."[20] And in her memoir from late 1990, Umm Mohammed wrote, "I ask my Muslim sisters to encourage their husbands and sons to continue with the jihad."[21]

Like his wife, Azzam appealed to all Muslim women to support the *mujahideen*. In Part Two of *Join the Caravan,* published in 1988, he provides sixteen motives for Muslims to fight, which are both for practical and ideological reasons,[22] but also addresses women in particular, who he views as the prime supporters of men. He states, "What is the matter with the mothers, that one of them does not send forward one of hers sons in the Path of Allah that he might be a pride for her in this world and a treasure for her in the Hereafter through her intercession?"[23] By declaring jihad as *fard*, Azzam transferred the balance from jihad *kifayah* (collective duty) to jihad as an individual duty.[24] This is a core message of female propagandists today.

THE ORIGINS OF VIOLENT WOMEN

Creating online connections with new members and deepening existing relationships allows radical women to develop kinship ties and establish a new family—a bond strengthened by ideals of sisterhood and a twisted form of belonging. The concept of sisterhood predates ISIS. In previous conflicts that predate al-Qaeda literature, women have consistently expressed their desire to unite and create a community of like-minded believers, romanticizing the terrorist family as self-sustaining and eternal.

Before the publication of print media, radical women expressed a desire to participate in violent jihad in television interviews and leading newspapers. During the Afghan jihad, some women backed the mujahideen, or male fighters, battling the former Soviet Union. In Urdu-language documents collected by the author from 1987-1996, articles about and for Muslim women in the Afghanistan-Pakistan region demonstrate the contribution that women can have in aiding male fighters. For example, an April 1987 issue of the *Al-Irshad* magazine features an article written by a woman *for* women. The female writer reminds women of their responsibility of taking part in jihad. She describes the poor conditions under which Muslim women live in Afghan society. She pleads for an active participation by women in the jihad movement, citing the example of the Prophet's female Companions, or *Suhabiat*. In a summer issue of the same magazine, an article titled "An Open Letter to Muslim Women" by an anonymous writer uses examples from Islamic history to prove that women played an active role in the early battles: the first Muslim women in 7th century Arabia fought alongside men to defend their honor, homes and holy Prophet. Citing history, the anonymous writer encouraged women in the region "to do the same as the need is urgent."[25] In the same time period, other articles called on women to send their sons to fight the enemies of Islam; scorned women for imitating Western culture and showing her outer beauty; and described the stages of martyrdom for both men and women.

In later years, radical women in Pakistan provided men sanctuary and raised their male children to join local extremist groups. Today, radical women are members of local Pakistani extremist groups, including Lashkar-e-Tayba and Hizb ul-Mujahideen, and extol jihad in their propaganda material.[26] A retired Brigadier of the Pakistani Army told the author, "These male cowards [extremists] are hiding behind the women to protect them, which is contrary to Islam." Based on a wide range of interviews with Pakistani authorities, local women are also radicalized by religious leaders to challenge the authority of the government.[27] Once radicalized, these women become more palatable to mainstream audiences and brand their message of resistance, rebellion, and rage against the enemies of their men.

In India and Pakistan, radical women are tools of terrorism, manipulated by men to motivate other women and insist on the need to unify when a pre-existing conflict exists. Because Kashmir is a hot-button issue in Pakistan, radical women can garner greater support from moderate communities when they reinforce the message of victimhood and expose trauma, tragedy and terrible acts committed by authorities against innocent civilians. The author's extensive interviews with women in the Kashmir valley suggest that women empower themselves when they issue statements, verbal and written, and distribute this material to communities already sensitized to the conflict. It is also possible that women have a greater ability to recruit other women when they apply associated symptoms of trauma, such as survivor's guilt, shame, loss, and helplessness, into their narrative.[28] In one case, an 18-year-old girl in Indian-held Kashmir told the author of her desire to join Laskhar-e-Tayba but was told that they did not need women to conduct attacks instead forcing the young woman to be a leading propagandist.[29]

Modern-day propagandists may believe that they are emulating the early Muslim women, who participated in different battles, fighting and dying alongside their men. Countless examples of these women are wrongly used by contemporary *muhajirat* to justify violent extremism. What is conveniently forgotten is that the first women warriors acted in *defense* of their religion, rather than exploit Islamic doctrine to engage and empower women worldwide. The original purpose of jihad, and by extension martyrdom, was to protect the Muslim community and the Prophet of Islam. Notable examples include Umm Umara, who treated the wounded, but as the army in the city of Mecca advanced to attack the Prophet, she ran to his defense, losing one arm and suffering eleven wounds in the Battle of Uhud (625 C.E.) Other women were known for their eulogies of war. They danced, beat their drums, and sang verses of encouragement.

> We are the daughters of the Morning Star.
> Our necks are adorned with pearls, our hair perfumed with musk.
> Fight fiercely and we will crush you in our arms.[30]

Women in the Prophet's family also participated in jihad. His youngest wife, Ayesha, led a battle and his grand daughter Zaynab bint Ali fought in the famous Battle of Karbala in what is modern-day Iraq. The Prophet's aunt, and sister of his beloved uncle Hamza, Safiya, was glorified when she killed a spy with a tent peg. Safiya also killed an enemy fighter and threw away his severed head into the enemy camp. It should be noted that the women referenced above are honored for defending their religion—unlike the radical women who attempt to constitute a monopoly in the marketplace of ideas with a restless enthusiasm and an indefatigable drive to support terrorist groups that operate outside of moderate, progressive Islamic doctrine.

FEMALE PROPAGANDISTS AND E-JIHAD

Contemporary radical women serve as an important propaganda tool. With words, they can mobilize support; serve as the mouthpiece of the terror organization; and recruit other women through media outlets and women-only gatherings. Acting as communication nodes, these women have a unique opportunity to augment facilitation, training and recruitment—the support of male propagandists and leaders made this possible for women. Common themes expressed in editorials and articles written by radical women are: the pursuit of jihad for the sake of Allah; to attain *shahada* (Arabic for martyrdom); to stand "shoulder to shoulder with [radical] men, supporting them, helping them, and backing them up;"[31] to educate and prepare their sons for jihad; and to be worthy of Paradise.

With the birth of Al-Qaeda, the late kingpin of terrorism Usama bin Laden extolled the role of the Muslim woman in jihad when he declared: "Our women had set a tremendous example of generosity in the case of Allah: they motivated and encouraged their sons, brothers, and husbands to fight [for Allah]." The former leader made it clear that Muslim women needed to be invited and included into the terrorist family to offer men moral and ideological support. The significance of inviting women into the al-Qaeda family increased the group's chances of survival, even when women were expendable. In a declassified intelligence assessment, the author wrote: "Women are a riding wave of al-Qaeda's success."[32]

As early as 2004, al-Qaeda released print magazines highlighting the roles of radical women. One of the first magazines was named *Al-Khansaa* after the Arab poetess whose original name is Tumadir bint Amru al-Harith bint al-Sharid. A convert to Islam in 7th century Arabia, al-Khansaa (Arabic for 'gazelle') wrote elegies for the dead and narrated her verses to Arabian tribes in public oral competitions. Before the rise of Islam, poetry recitation was highly valued. She was also known for encouraging men in her family to join the battlefield, for which al-Khansaa gained notoriety in her community, including her four sons (all died fighting for Islam). On the news of their death, or martyrdom, al-Khansaa is reported to have said, "Praise be to Allah who honored me with their martyrdom. I pray for Allah to let me join them in heaven." In al-Qaeda's *Al-Khansaa* magazine, guidance is provided to Muslim women on how to raise children as well as physical training exercises for women, should they take part in fighting. For example, one article reads: "The blood of our husbands and the body parts of our children are our sacrificial offering," emphasizing the supportive role of radical women in violent groups.

Two years later in July 2006, Umayma, the wife of the veteran terrorist leader in Iraq, Abu Mus'ab al-Zarqawi posted a letter on the Mujahideen Shura Council website, calling on Muslims everywhere to defend the honor of their husbands and participate in jihad. In December 2009, a document by Umayma entitled "Letter to My Muslim Sisters" (risala ila al-akhawat al-muslimat) encouraged Muslim women to observe Islam (i.e., raise children in the path of God) as well as inspire them to fight with courage, as women did in the time of their Prophet in the early battles of Islam.[33] While Umayma does not openly tell female radicals to take part in terrorist operations, she does encourage their contribution:

> jihad [today] is an individual duty incumbent upon every Muslim man and woman, but the path of fighting is not easy for women, for it requires a male companion with whom it is lawful for a woman to be...We put ourselves in the

service of the jihadis, we carry out what they ask, whether in supporting them financially, serving their [practical] needs, supplying them with information, opinions, partaking in fighting or even [volunteering to carry out] a martyrdom operation... Our principal role [sic.] is to protect the jihadis [through] bringing up their children, [managing] their homes, and [keeping] their secrets.

A 40-year-old Jordanian national, Umayma protested the death of her husband in an online communiqué when he was killed by an American airstrike. She called for revenge, and declared: "We are all Zarqawi." Umayma intended to provoke Muslim men by shaming them, insisting that they commit terror attacks to avenge her husband's death. It should be noted that women also detonated during the Iraq conflict. At the start of the war in Iraq, some Muslim girls and women strapped on the bomb and committing more than 50 suicide attacks across the country. Among them was Iraqi-born Sajida al-Rishawi, who accompanied her husband in Jordan to attack a wedding party at the Radisson hotel: she was the first al-Qaeda woman to be captured alive until her hanging by the Jordanian government in 2015. While dangerous, the female bombers are a minority compared to the female propagandists that could number in the hundreds—the women charged with sending out effective messages to a wide target audience are arguably more deadly than the small number of female bombers.

Around the same period, a Moroccan-born Belgian Muslim woman, Malika al-Aroud, self-published her memoir, *Les soldats de lumiere* (French for Soldiers of Light). The author received a copy of the book from CNN's Paul Cruinshank, who profiled the female propagandist in a *Marie Claire* magazine article titled "Love in the Time of Terror." Cruinshank described al-Aroud as a single mom married to Abdessattar who died in Afghanistan while committing a terrorist attack. In his interview with al-Aroud, the radical woman explained her return to Islam: "I heard the Arabic call of prayer, and I felt something very strong in my heart telling me to wake up and return...I discovered that God's forgiveness is immense."[34] In her book, she described her love for God, *Sa Lumiere* (French for His Light). For years, al-Aroud used the Internet to rally women behind her cause, sharing her personal story: highlighting her status as a martyr's widow; convincing women their responsibility to actively support jihad; and inspiring men to commit attacks. In a public statement, al-Aroud said: "I have a weapon. It's to write. It's to speak out. That's my jihad. You can do many things with words. Writing is also a bomb." On May 12, 2009, days after the article was published, al-Aroud was arrested for marrying into the al-Qaeda family.

Religious enablers of jihad permitted the wives of al-Qaeda men to play a wider role in violent jihad. The late al-Qaeda leader in the Arabian Peninsula, Yusuf Iyari a.k.a. Swift Sword, authored a book called *The Role of Women in the Jihad Against the Enemies*[35] in which he begins with the following: "My honored sister: Indeed for you is an important and great role, and you must rise and fulfill your obligatory role in Islam's confrontation of the new Crusade being waged by all the countries of the world against Islam and the Muslims. I will address you in these papers... So listen, may Allah protect and preserve you." He described the current state of the *Ummah* (Arabic for Muslim worldwide community) as disgraced and humiliation—the only escape, according to Iyari, is to "return to jihad and the love of fighting in the Path of Allah, and the abandonment of the *Dunya* (Arabic for life on earth) and its adornments." Iyari's respect and love for Muslim women are made clear in his words—she is the "cradle of the men." Iyari recognized that women could leverage their gender and simultaneously have innovative advantages and capacities to expand the extremist propaganda network. He acknowledged that "the saying behind every great man stands a woman was true for Muslim women at these times, for behind every great Mujahid stood a woman." While there have been other male religious enablers of violent jihad, Iyari was arguably among the first male writers to call on women to join the terrorist movement. In time, radical women would heed his call and publish their own material.

Years later, in 2011, a glossy women's magazine named *Al Shamikah* (Arabic for 'majestic woman), was released by the Al-Fajr Media Center in Saudi Arabia. The magazine's Glamour-style stories targeted radical women, featuring on its cover a clip-art illustration of a veiled woman next to a gun, and articles titled "Meeting a Jihad Wife" and "Pages From the Pen of a Female Jihadist" which appear in bold-faced type. Other articles stressed a Muslim woman's appearance—what to wear and how to maintain beautiful skin by staying indoors.[36] The editor of the magazine, Saleh Youssef, said the objective of the magazine was to educate women and involve them in the war against the enemies of Islam. He declared: " Because women constitute half of the population—and one might even say that they are the population since they give birth to the next generation—the enemies of Islam are bent on preventing the Muslim woman from knowing the truth about her religion and her role, since they know all too well what would happen if women entered the field of jihad." Earlier al-Qaeda magazines, *Sada al-Malahim* (The Voice of Battle) and *Sada al-Jihad* (The Voice of Jihad), also encouraged women to join the terrorist cause.

Given the current threat environment, the women of ISIS have gained international attention. Writing behind-the-screens, these female propagandists are viewed by their followers as credible messengers, speaking out in volumes about life, death, marriage, martyrdom, as well as other how-to topics: how to live when your husband dies; how to fit in when a woman goes to Raqqa, the ISIS-controlled city in Syria; how to behave with other women; how to please your new husband; and how to be a pure Muslim woman. The latter concept correlates with the idea that good Muslim women are chaste, often reflected in the concept of "the image of the pure nation," a theme echoed by scholars who assess that national struggles and programs use women to "internalize the desirable national image of mother and wife, of desexualized members of the community."[37]

Outside the Muslim world, such as within the Catholic community in Ireland, women have "symbolically represented the purity and tradition of the country," and encouraged to embody the "ideal of Mary [the mother of Jesus] in their own 'essence.'"[38] This expression can be applied to Muslim women, who are raised to emulate the actions, behaviors, and practices of the first Muslim women in Arabia, including the women in the Prophet's family. The Iranian Shia political philosopher Ali Shariati, in his book *Fatima Is Fatima,* glorifies the Prophet's daughter as the symbol of piety.[39] The "mothers of the believers" is a reference to the Prophet's female family members and an honorific title that the *muhajirat* desire.

A brief look at ISIS propagandists reveals their simplicity and desire for life after death. Under the cover of Umm Layth, Scottish-born Aqsa Mahmood maintains a blog titled "Diary of a Muhajirah," in which she proudly tweets about the Afterlife. In 2014, she posted: "My sisters. We made *hijrah* [migration] together. May Allah grant us *shahada* [martyrdom] & unite us in *Jannah* [heaven]." Another English-speaking ISIS woman, under the guise of Al-Brittaniyah, posted: "May Allah grant all the wives of the Mujahideen *Sabr* [patience] and re-unite them in the Highest *Jannah* with their Husbands." Dressed in a *niqab* or face-veil, another Muslim woman brandishing a Kalashnikov declared: "I know what I'm doing. Paradise has a price and I hope this will be the price of Paradise."[40]

Regarding marriage and love, the women of ISIS fail to recognize that their relationship may not be real or long-term. A report by the Quilliam Foundation indicates that some women are captivated by an imaginary future. "The promise of an Islamist utopia" charms many of these girls, according to Haris Rafiz,[41] the managing director of Quilliam. A former radical woman told BBC news that she wanted a "piece of eye candy" and was scouting the Internet for radical men with good looks—men who are "really, really attractive." Another ISIS woman, writing under the name Umm Waqqas, may be among the few women who know how to make a marriage work. "Patience to deal with everyday struggles." Her overall message can be summarized in this one tweet: "There's no such thing as Prince Charming. It's actually fictional, but u can mold ur spouse into becoming ur everything I've ever wanted." But even Umm Waqqas knows that her marriage to an ISIS fighter is anything short of a fantasy.[42]

Not surprisingly, many radical women seeking to marry men online do not understand Islam. Given the women's ignorance of the faith, women are easily lured into the scripture that radical men reimagine and reinterpret; principles of honor, marriage and martyrdom are extolled and radical women are therefore easily persuaded to accept a distorted reading of the Quran and Islamic history. To be fair, ISIS is not the only group to espouse imaginary rulings on Islam to advance their strategic and tactical goals. During the Iraq war, various Islamic chat rooms and forums compelled women to join. The Abu al-Boukhari Islamic Network, for example, told women that because Islam is under attack, they are obligated to defend their faith and the men. For radical women, ignorance is *not* bliss. One ISIS female recruit, using the moniker Umm Lath, wrote: "Women are not equal to men. It can never be. Men are the leaders and women are [so] special that Allah has given them entire chapter in the Quran," a reference to *Sura al-Nisa* (Arabic for The Verse on Women). Failing to understand and study Islam denies these women their rights. Instead, radical women under the tutelage of ISIS choose a life of austerity, patriarchal authority, and an absence of normalcy.

COUNTER-MESSAGING

Successful counter-messaging campaigns depend heavily on former radicals, mostly men, who are willing to work with local groups and governments to disrupt existing radical networks and prevent vulnerable individuals from choosing violent extremism. The author's personal interactions with former radicals suggest that there often exists a pre-event factor that influenced entry into a terrorist group. These factors could include: previous exposure to severe adverse life events; earlier depression or anxiety; family instability; absence of social support; childhood trauma or victimization; multiple earlier losses of people or possessions, such as one's home; and age. These predispositions are generally associated with adults who have been exposed to stress-related incidents.

While former radicals do not speak openly about a trigger event, it is important to recognize that the process of radicalization and de-radicalization are effective when taking a case-by-case approach, even when common narratives exist among defectors—these could include a bipolar view of Islam (Sunni versus Shia); exposure to human tragedy and trauma; and/or dissatisfaction with living under the rule of terrorist organizations. A study by London's Quilliam Foundation analyzed the in-and-out journeys of extremists, focusing on their emotional and cognitive behavior to develop counter-extremism strategies to prevent radicalization.[43]

If perceived injustice and grievances are addressed, will radical women stop writing? Studies by Dr. Jessica Stern and Dr. Robert Pape emphasize common distresses among Muslims when there is a narrative of victimization and a vicious cycle of violence in given conflicts.[44] Some of these grievances are decades or centuries old but continue to empower, enthrall, and possibly enslave Muslim women into believing that violence is the *only* alternative available to affect change. There is no evidence that removing local and global grievances will dissuade radical women from distributing messages on violent extremism, especially if other pre-event factors exist to encourage women to write. Another important area of research that profiles the circumstance may be a useful mechanism—especially the conditions under which women live—to understand if there are local grievances, such as humiliation, alienation, rage, or (perceived) occupation, which could give rise to terrorist involvement.[45]

To guide counter-messaging, Islamic history and scripture needs to be rightly appropriated. A majority of Muslim scholars reject the use of violence, arguing that the Prophet of Islam prohibited taking one's life. According to the Prophet, violence and suicide prohibited a believer from entering paradise (i.e. the oral tradition states that the gates of Paradise will be closed forever to anyone who takes his/her own life). And yet the literature of martyrdom propagated by radical men and women argue the opposite. By carefully selecting the word "martyrdom" (literally to bear witness and to sacrifice for faith), religious radicals contend that violence is legitimate, legal, and laudable. Martyrdom is therefore necessary, since it connotes the sacrifice of the perpetrator to choose the rewards of the afterlife over the shortcomings of *this* life.[46]

Countering this argument requires re-explaining the narrative of life and death in Islam, focusing instead on the purpose of life and the meaning of death. Re-explaining and raising awareness of Islamic doctrine and practice can help women foster a new identity, making them proud and happy-to-be-alive, rather than distressed and depressed because of the myth and fear that Islam is in a state of decline; Islam is under attack; or that Muslims are continually threatened by the West.

In the same way, addressing ideological disagreements among global radical men and women is necessary to weaken their ideological outlook, while exposing them to teachings of mercy, peace, and compassion supported by verses in the Quran and the *Hadith* (Arabic for oral traditions). Recognizing that ideological divisions exist even among moderate Muslims, the counter-messaging campaign is arguably effective when there is agreement on alternative narratives. Currently, there are a wide range of narratives that are distributed by Muslim-led groups in various communities in the West and abroad: the use of film, including animation; educational guides for school teachers and parents; training for families on indicators of youth radicalization; and online campaigns. While it may be too soon to measure the results of these campaigns, there is a worldwide awareness that countering the narrative of ISIS and like-minded groups is essential.

FINAL THOUGHTS

Women serve as messengers for radical groups. In service to the terrorist organization and its domineering men, women write. They send out a plethora of messages on social media sites to raise awareness, recruit *other* women as well as Muslim men, rationalize violence, and reinforce their religious beliefs. Because women are not historically operational actors, writing can be their greatest weapon—and service—to male-dominated terror groups.

Additionally, it is argued that men fight wars for the right to speak, to have ideas, to have value, and to be a human being. But the same logic fails to apply to radical women. Radical men are quick to control the women they invite into their organizations, except in writing. ISIS men have denied Muslim women their basic rights in Islam: the right to dress freely; to step outside the home; the right to work; the right to learn in a university; and the right to speak in non-religious language. In short, these men have failed to respect Muslim women as equal to men in the eyes of God.

Creative strategies are needed to counter the persecution of women under ISIS's old-school authoritarian rule. First, restoring Muslim women's rights and strengthening the family's ability to communicate with each member can alleviate the need for some women to join violent extremism. Secondly, re-teaching Islam is one part of a wider strategy to degrade ISIS's ability to prey on women, who are uninformed and ignorant of the teachings of their faith. The author's initiative, labeled "Families First," is designed to value each member of the Muslim family and reward women (and girls) for their duties, roles and responsibilities, with educational resources, training, and other support mechanisms. Third, promoting a strong sense of tradition and history is equally important—Islamic cultures honor their place in the world and conform to certain norms that exist in collectivist societies, where expectations of each individual in the familial group is defined in relation to the group.[47] Ultimately, building strong families and offering support services to those living in conflict will enable women to avoid the snare of violent extremism and help them lead healthy, normal lives.

NOTES

1. A comparable model of the Four Rs can be found in other scholarly work, including Mia Bloom's *Bombshell.* The author first presented the model to U.S. Government audiences in August 2005.
    2. Andrew Silke, "The Psychology of Suicide Terrorism," in Silke (ed.), *Terrorists, Victims, and Society,* (Sussex, England: Wiley, 2003), 105-107.
    3. For background of these factors, see Silke, "Becoming a Terrorist," in Silke (ed.), *Terrorists, Victims, and Society,* 37-51.
    4. John Horgan, *The Psychology of Terrorism* (London: Routledge, 2005 and 2008).
    5. Jerold Post, "The Psychological Roots of Terrorism," in *Addressing the Causes of Terrorism: The Club de Madrid Series on Democracy and Terrorism,* Vol. 1 (Madrid: Club de

Madrid, 2005); Jerold Post, E. Sprinzak, and L. Denny "The Terrorists in Their Own Words: Interviews with 35 Incarcerated Middle Eastern Terrorists," *Terrorism and Political Violence*, Vol. 15, No. 1 (2003), 171-184; and Horgan, *The Psychology of Terrorism.*

6. See Mia Bloom, "Mother. Daughter. Sister. Bomber," in *Bulletin of the Atomic Scientists* (November-December 2005).

7. Mia Bloom, "Motivations for Suicide Terrorism," *Root Causes of Suicide Terrorism,* Ami Pedhazur (ed.), (New York: Routledge, 2006), 39.

8. Saltman, Erin and Smith, Melanie, "Till Martyrdom Do Us Part," The Institute for Strategic Dialogue, (UK: 2015), 10.

9. Ibid, 11.

10. Laden with inaccurate perceptions, jihad today is synonymous with "terrorism," "extremism," and "radicalism." No other term in the Muslim vocabulary has been flagrantly misunderstood in the West than jihad—a word that has been harmed by an unsound meaning of "holy war." Imam Muhammad Magid of ADAMS, a mosque and community center in Sterling, Virginia, says, "Nowhere in the Qur'an will you find holy war attributed to jihad." Correcting the misconceptions and the biases attached to the term requires a brief explanation of what it is, and what it is not.

11. Fatoohi, 67

12. Lewis, 116

13. Iyyari was killed in Saudi Arabia in June 2004. For background texts on jihad, see Jalal Abualrub, *Holy Wars, Crusades, Jihad* (Orlando: Madinah Publishers, 2002) and Rudolph Peters, *Jihad in Classical and Modern Islam: A Reader* (Princeton: Markus Wiener, 1996).

14. Abualrub, 78-79

15. Dr. Maher Hathout, senior advisor of the Muslim Public Affairs Council (MPAC) in Washington, DC, says, "Historically, fighting back against aggressors [the pagan Quraysh tribe] was prohibited during the thirteen years of the Meccan period ... [but] after the migration to Medina and the establishment of the Islamic state, Muslims were concerned with how to defend themselves against aggression from their enemies." After thirteen years of persecution and living in exile, the permission to fight enabled the early Muslims to protect themselves against the Quraysh and other enemies anxious to destroy the Islamic community. For background, see Abualrub, *Holy Wars, Crusades, Jihad* and Peters, *Jihad in Classical and Modern Islam: A Reader.*

16. Aslan, 86.

17. Azzam notes in the article that Bin Baz "declared in the mosque of Ibn Ladna in Jeddah and in the large mosque of Riyadh that Jihad with your person today is *Fard Ayn* [global obligation]." The fatwa was also signed by other Saudi-based clerics, including Sheikh Mohammed Bin Salah Bin Uthaimin.

18. Sheikh Abdullah Azzam, "Join the Caravan," *Al Jihad,* December 1988, 23.

19. Al-Shafey, Mohammad, *Al-Sharq Al-Awsati Interviews Umm Mohammed: The Wife of Bin Laden's Spiritual Mentor,* April 30, 2006.

20. Presentation by the author to a U.S. Government audience, 2013.

21. Sheikh Abdullah Azzam, *Al Jihad,* Issue 7 (November-December 1990).

22. Azzam's sixth reason for waging jihad is to establish a solid foundation as a base of Islam; he writes, "This homeland [Afghanistan] will not come about without an organized Islamic movement," ("Join the Caravan," 14) By stressing victory in Afghanistan, Azzam's goal was to "change the tide of the battle, from an Islamic battle in one country, to an Islamic World Jihad movement." This would suggest that Azzam believed in spreading Islam, although his actions—and the bulk of his writing—indicated his focus was winning the battle in Afghanistan.

23. Sheikh Abdullah Azzam, "Join the Caravan, Part II," *Al Jihad,* 1988, 27.

24. In contemporary Islamic reform movements, the founder of Wahhabism in present-day Saudi Arabia, Muhammad Abd al Wahhab, first proclaimed the idea of jihad *kifayah,* but set jihad within limits rather than a blanket prescription for violence. Abdul Wahhab set limitations on violence as well as the killing and destruction of property. For a complete biography, see Natana J. DeLong-Bas, *Wahhabi Islam* (New York: Oxford University Press, 2004). Contrary to accepted Western analysis, Abdul Wahhab never discussed martyrdom, paradise, or heaven-

ly rewards in his writings on jihad; instead, he promulgated the sanctity of life, which is best reflected in his work, *Kitab al-Tawhid* (Book of Monotheism), colored with Qur'anic verses and *hadith*.

25. Documents collected in Pakistan for a research project for the Rand Corporation. Translation was provided by linguist Afzaal Mahmood.

26. Ali, Farhana, "Dressed in Black: A Look at Pakistan's Radical Women," The Jamestown Foundation, Volume 5, Issue 8 (26 April 2007).

27. Author's interviews conducted with Pakistani military officers and government officials.

28. Interviews with women in Kashmir are compiled in the author's non-fiction book, *Secrets of the Kashmir Valley*, (Pharos: India, 2016).

29. Interview described in detail in "Bomb Girl" in *Secrets of the Kashmir Valley*.

30. Jennifer Heath, *The Scimitar and the Veil*, (HiddenSpring: New Jersey, 2004), 209-212.

31. "Women Must Participate in Jihad," *Al-Qaeda Magazine*, 7 September 2004.

32. The findings of the assessment was published as "Rocking the Cradle to Rocking the World" in *The Journal of International Women's Studies* by Farhana Ali

33. Umaya al-Zawahiri, "Women's Role in Jihad," *Jihadica*, 26 February 2010.

34. Paul Cruinshank, "Love in the Time of Terror," *Marie Claire*, May 2009.

35. Yusuf al-Iyari, *The Role of the Women in Fighting the Enemies*, At-Tibyan Publications, acquired by an internal U.S. Government source.

36. Caitlin Dickson, "Al-Qaeda's New Women's Magazine," *The Wire*, 14 March 2011.

37. For background, see Julie Mostov, "Sexing the nation/desexing the body," in *Gender Ironies of Nationalism: Sexing the Nation*, Tamar Mayer, ed., (New York: Routledge, 2000), 103.

38. Angela K. Martin, "Death of a nation in Ireland," in *Gender Ironies of Nationalism: Sexing the Nation*, 67-70.

39. Reza Aslan makes the argument that Fatima was used to defy the Western image of womanhood. He discounts Shariati's approach and states that the "traditional colonial image of the veiled Muslim woman as the sheltered, docile sexual property of her husband is just as misleading and simpleminded as the postmodernist image of the veil as the emblem of female freedom and empowerment from Western cultural hegemony." See Aslan, *No God But God: The Origins, Evolution and Future of Islam* (London: Arrow Books, 2006), 73-74.

40. Farhana Qazi, "The Modern Mujahidaat: What Women Want When They Join ISIS–Part I," *Levant News*, 5 March 2015.

41. Siva Kumar, "Girls Are Being Lured Through Handsome 'ISIS Candy' Men," *News Everyday*, 4 March 2015.

42. Farhana Qazi, "The Modern Mujahidaat: What Women Do Not See When They Join ISIS – Part II," *The Levant*, 6 March 2015.

43. Ruth Manning and Courtney La Bau, *In and Out of Extremism: How Quilliam Helped 10 Former Far-Right and Islamists Change*, Quilliam Foundation.

44. Robert Pape, *Dying to Win: The Strategic Logic of Suicide Terrorism* (New York, NY: Random House, 2005); Jessica Stern, *Terror in the Name of God: Why Religious Militants Kill*, (New York, NY: Harper Collins, 2003)

45. Terrorism expert Jessica Stern addresses these grievances in her book *Terror in the Name of God* (New York: Harper Collins, 2003).

46. For a genre of literature on the benefits of martyrdom (*shahadat*), see essays by Shia scholars Ayatullah Mahmud Taleqani, Ayatullah Murtada Mutahhari, and Dr. Ali Shari'ati in Mehdi Abedi and Gary Legenhausen (eds.), *Jihad and Shahadat: Struggle and Martyrdom in Islam* (Houston, TX: Institute for Research and Islamic Studies, 1986). Sunni scholarship offers more diverse writings on the subject, including militant and moderate authors; for example, consider Sayyid Qutb, "Jihad in the Cause of God," in *Milestones* (Cedar Rapids, IA: Mother Mosque Foundation, 1993), 53-76; Yusuf al-Qaradawi, "The Prophet Muhammad as a Jihad Model," *Middle East Media Research Institute Special Dispatch* No. 246, 24 July 2001; Majid Khadduri, *War and Peace in the Law of Islam, Book 2: The Law of War: The Jihad* (Baltimore: Johns Hopkins University Press, 1955), 49-73.

47. Kritika Kongsompong, "Consumer Diversity in Multicultural Arenas: An Investigation of Social Influences Between Asians and Westerners," *International Business and Economics Research Journal,* 5:12 (2006): 55-64.

About the Authors

Editor: Ajit Maan, Ph.D. is an internationally recognized security and defense analyst and narrative strategist. She developed the ground-breaking theory of *Internarrative Identity*, a road map for resilient identity created out of personal and cultural conflict. Her work has had far-reaching implications for conflict resolution and community engagement in hostile environments. Dr. Maan's recent work on terrorist recruitment narratives, and her book *Counter-terrorism: Narrative Strategies* focuses on deconstructing dominant and coercive narratives and demonstrates how certain narrative structures lend themselves to manipulation and how the weaknesses of those structures can be exploited. Dr. Maan is the President and founder of Narrative Strategies, a think-tank consultancy focused on the non-kinetic aspects of counter-terrorism and asymmetric warfare; she is a partner at WeSolve, Inc.; Affiliate Faculty at Center for Narrative Conflict Resolution at George Mason University; and Affiliate Faculty of Interdisciplinary Doctoral Studies at the Union Institute and University.

An Indian military veteran, Brigadier Amar Cheema, earned his MSc and M. Phil in Defense and Strategic Studies from the University of Madras. After a distinguished 34 year military career, he became a Senior Research Fellow with India's premier Think Tank The United Service Institution (USI), and remains a Consultant Editor with the *Indian Defense Review* (IDR). Post retirement, he took over as the first Chief Knowledge Officer and created the Knowledge Center of Shoolini University. His current mission is to give shape and direction to the RIMT University in Punjab as its first Registrar, Director of the Dron Knowledge Center and Center of Strategic Studies (CSS). Author of *The Crimson Chinar—The Kashmir Conflict: A Politico-Military Perspective*, an analytical account of the conflict from its genesis to the current stage, Amar is a proponent of applying humane solutions to mitigate conflict. He writes on issues of strategic import concerning national and international security and military history, most of which are available on the net. He lives with his wife in Chandigarh, India.

Paul Cobaugh is a recently retired US Army Warrant Officer. Mr. Cobaugh spent the past decade working for the US Special Operations Command (USSOCOM) in the Civil Affairs and Information Operations fields. His experience includes seven deployments with most of the time spent in Iraq and Afghanistan. Mr. Cobaugh's specialties while serving as an Information Operations practitioner for USSOCOM included effective engagement with indigenous populations and the planning and execution of comprehensive Information Operations strategies in support of select USSOCOM forces.

Christopher Holshek is an international peace and security consultant on civil-military and peace operations education and training. Recent projects include a National Defense University Defense Minerva grant project to leverage social science research for Joint Professional Military Education to facilitate Training Transformation and enable the Joint Force to better conduct irregular warfare. A member of the US Global Leadership Coalition's "Veterans for Smart Power," he is a retired US Army Civil Affairs officer with three decades of civil-military operations experience at the strategic, operational, and tactical levels in joint, interagency, and multinational settings across the full range of operations, including: EUCOM/SHAPE Military Representative at USAID; Senior US Military Observer and Chief of Civil-Military Coordination in the UN Mission in Liberia; and, command of the first CA battalion to deploy to Iraq in support of Army, Marine and British forces. He helped develop civil-military policy and doctrine for the US Army, DoD, NATO, and the UN as well as partner nations. A rare American who served with the UN in civilian and military capacities, he is a Senior Fellow at the Alliance for Peacebuilding, a senior advisor in the UN Association of the USA, and a Director in the Civil Affairs Association, for which he organizes annual Symposia and Roundtables and edits the annual Civil Affairs Issue Papers . He also writes extensively on peace and security, strategy, civil-military relations, and peace operations, and his articles have appeared in *Foreign Policy* and *The Huffington Post*, among others. His new book, *Travels with Harley – Journeys in Search of Personal and National Identity*, is the basis of his National Service Ride initiative to promote better citizenship, service, and social responsibility in and beyond America.

Lieutenant Colonel Chris Mayer, Ph.D. is the Associate Dean for Strategy, Policy, and Assessment and an assistant professor of philosophy at the United States Military Academy. He served as Academy Professor in the Department of English and Philosophy at the USMA from 2010-2015. He graduated with a Bachelor of Science degree from West Point in 1993 and entered the Quartermaster Branch of the US Army. As a Quartermaster and Force Management officer, he served in operational assignments at Fort Campbell, KY; Camp Zama, Japan; and Fort Monroe, VA. Lieutenant Colonel Mayer deployed to Iraq from 2006 to 2007, and was assigned to the Multinational Security Transition Command, Iraq. During this assignment, he facilitated the organization and equipping of the Iraqi Civil Security Forces. He has a Master of Public Administration from Murray State University, a Master of Arts in Philosophy from Virginia Tech, and a Doctorate in Philosophy from the University of Virginia. He is a member of the American Philosophical Association, the American Association of Philosophy Teachers, and the Association of American Colleges and Universities. He teaches courses in moral and political philosophy, ethics of war, philosophy of religion, and Eastern Thought, and he has published in the areas of the ethics of war, character, social ontology, and teaching and learning.

Eirini Patsea is an attorney and Cultural Diplomacy specialist. Her work has been featured in *moderndiplomacy.eu* and *thedailyjournalist.com*. She has gained her most valuable working experiences through volunteering in a local Greek NGO providing Greek language lessons and legal representation to refugee women and children. When she's not hustling her way through the Conflict Assessment and Intervention Planning "elite" circles, you can find her reading about international politics, writing about her take on international politics and watching documentaries about *Ancient Aliens* without a trace of shame.

Farhana Qazi is a scholar and speaker on conflicts in the Islamic world. She received the 21st Century Leader Award by the National Committee on American Foreign Policy (NCAFP) for her service to the US Government, and the Humanitarian Award from her alma mater in Texas. Ms. Qazi has published widely in mainstream news outlets and foreign policy journals. Her short articles have appeared in *Newsweek, Reuters, Washington Post, The Wall Street Journal, Big Think, The International Herald Tribune, The Islamic Monthly, Levant News,* and more. She has appeared in every major news network, including CNN, BBC, FOX, Bloomberg, Al-Jazeera, PBS, NPR, C-Span and Voice of America. She received her Bachelor of Arts at Southwestern University in Texas and a Masters in Security Policy Studies at The George Washington University in Washington, D.C. She is the author of *Secrets of the Valley: A Personal Journey to the War in Kashmir Between India and Pakistan.*

Printed in Great Britain
by Amazon